Readings *for* Funerals

Readings
for Funerals

Compiled by
MARK OAKLEY

First published in Great Britain in 2015

Society for Promoting Christian Knowledge
36 Causton Street
London SW1P 4ST
www.spckpublishing.co.uk

For copyright acknowledgements, please see p. 226.

Every effort has been made to seek permission to use copyright
material reproduced in this book. The publisher apologizes for those
cases where permission might not have been sought and, if notified,
will formally seek permission at the earliest opportunity.

British Library Cataloguing-in-Publication Data
A catalogue record for this book is available from
the British Library

ISBN 978-0-281-07180-7

Typeset by Graphicraft Limited, Hong Kong
Manufacture managed by Jellyfish
First printed in Great Britain by CPI Group
Subsequently digitally printed in Great Britain

Produced on paper from sustainable forests

In grateful memory
of
John Slater
– priest and friend –

As far as we can discern, the sole purpose
of human existence is to kindle a light in
the darkness of mere being

Carl Jung

Contents

Poems and reflections

Hymns

Introduction

> Though lovers be lost love shall not;
> And death shall have no dominion.
>
> Dylan Thomas

One of the sermons I am able to remember well was given in St Paul's Cathedral by the then Dean, Eric Evans. It was Easter Day and the Dean was frail and, we now know, near to his own death. He used a poem, 'And Death Shall Have No Dominion', by the Welsh poet Dylan Thomas to help him preach the Easter gospel, and the strength of Eric's faith came through an inspirited and resonant reading of it from the pulpit. I can hear him now:

> They shall have stars at elbow and foot;
> Though they go mad they shall be sane,
> Though they sink through the sea they shall
>   rise again;
> Though lovers be lost love shall not;
> And death shall have no dominion.

The splash of these words caused ripples to head out towards the shores of the congregation that Easter Sunday, carrying the Easter hope in fresh and startling ways. I remain profoundly grateful.

This book is a modest collection of readings, some biblical and others not, which might be appropriate to be heard at a funeral. The emotional currents of a funeral are strong: grief, maybe anger, thanksgiving, guilt, celebration, confusion. These need to find a voice through bereavement and sometimes it is helpful for poetry to express those first waves of a grieving community's feelings and thoughts. At a Christian funeral it is also essential that this is not just an outpouring of self-expression but is rather an expression of human reality at such times, given space in the act of worship that commends a loved person to our creator. That expressiveness is placed within the context of Christian hope that in life and in death God is the home where all our loose ends, all our contradictions and unresolved identities, find a home.

If suitable readings cannot be found here then I hope the book will prompt readers to search further to find the right words, maybe even inspiring them to write their own. The Irish poet Michael Longley once said that 'if prose is a river, poetry is a fountain', and at a funeral the refreshment this fountain can give is vital. The popularity of the psalms, those ancient poems of faith, show this clearly – many of them expressing a dark and despairing dialogue with God through hurt and loss. Many of the more recent poems here are in the same tradition and some are more able to express gratitude and trust.

When I was a young priest I was asked to preside at a funeral of an actor. His daughter told me that as a young girl she would get upset when her father had to go away on tours and to film locations. Every time he knew he was going away for a long period he would tell her he loved her and then took out a five pound note from his pocket. He tore it in two and gave half to her, telling her 'This is to promise you that we'll be together soon and, when we are, we'll put the two halves together and you can spend it to celebrate.' As I stood with her, years later, next to the open coffin of her father, she took half a five pound note and gently placed it into his hand.

That act of love, shaped with both sadness and hope, is similar to the task crafted words might take on at a funeral. The space placed around the words in a poem is as important as the words themselves. I hope that this collection will allow those spaces to reach the hearts of those who have the privilege of commending a loved one to God, the God who is the great magnetism of mystery and the inviting harbour of love.

Mark Oakley
St Paul's Cathedral

Bible readings

Job 19.23–27

O that my words were written down!
   O that they were inscribed in a book!
O that with an iron pen and with lead
   they were engraved on a rock for ever!
For I know that my Redeemer lives,
   and that at the last he will stand upon the earth;
and after my skin has been thus destroyed,
   then in my flesh I shall see God,
whom I shall see on my side,
   and my eyes shall behold, and not another.

Psalm 15

O LORD, who may abide in your tent?
   Who may dwell on your holy hill?

Those who walk blamelessly, and do what is right,
   and speak the truth from their heart;
who do not slander with their tongue,
   and do no evil to their friends,
   nor take up a reproach against their neighbours;
in whose eyes the wicked are despised,
   but who honour those who fear the LORD;
who stand by their oath even to their hurt;
who do not lend money at interest,
   and do not take a bribe against the innocent.

Those who do these things shall never be moved.

Psalm 23

The LORD is my shepherd, I shall not want.
   He makes me lie down in green pastures;
he leads me beside still waters;
   he restores my soul.
He leads me in right paths
   for his name's sake.

Even though I walk through the darkest valley,
   I fear no evil;
for you are with me;
   your rod and your staff –
   they comfort me.

You prepare a table before me
   in the presence of my enemies;
you anoint my head with oil;
   my cup overflows.
Surely goodness and mercy shall follow me
   all the days of my life,
and I shall dwell in the house of the LORD
   my whole life long.

Psalm 27

The LORD is my light and my salvation;
    whom shall I fear?
The LORD is the stronghold of my life;
    of whom shall I be afraid?

When evildoers assail me
    to devour my flesh –
my adversaries and foes –
    they shall stumble and fall.

Though an army encamp against me,
    my heart shall not fear;
though war rise up against me,
    yet I will be confident.

One thing I asked of the LORD,
    that will I seek after:
to live in the house of the LORD
    all the days of my life,
to behold the beauty of the LORD,
    and to inquire in his temple.

For he will hide me in his shelter
    in the day of trouble;
he will conceal me under the cover of his tent;
    he will set me high on a rock.

Now my head is lifted up
    above my enemies all around me,
and I will offer in his tent
    sacrifices with shouts of joy;
I will sing and make melody to the LORD.

Hear, O LORD, when I cry aloud,
    be gracious to me and answer me!
'Come,' my heart says, 'seek his face!'
    Your face, LORD, do I seek.
    Do not hide your face from me.

Do not turn your servant away in anger,
    you who have been my help.
Do not cast me off, do not forsake me,
    O God of my salvation!
If my father and mother forsake me,
    the LORD will take me up.

Teach me your way, O LORD,
    and lead me on a level path
    because of my enemies.
Do not give me up to the will of my adversaries,
    for false witnesses have risen against me,
    and they are breathing out violence.

I believe that I shall see the goodness of the LORD
    in the land of the living.
Wait for the LORD;
    be strong, and let your heart take courage;
    wait for the LORD!

Psalm 42

As a deer longs for flowing streams,
  so my soul longs for you, O God.
My soul thirsts for God,
  for the living God.
When shall I come and behold
  the face of God?
My tears have been my food
  day and night,
while people say to me continually,
  'Where is your God?'

These things I remember,
  as I pour out my soul:
how I went with the throng,
  and led them in procession to the house of God,
with glad shouts and songs of thanksgiving,
  a multitude keeping festival.
Why are you cast down, O my soul,
  and why are you disquieted within me?
Hope in God; for I shall again praise him,
  my help and my God.

My soul is cast down within me;
  therefore I remember you
from the land of Jordan and of Hermon,
  from Mount Mizar.
Deep calls to deep
  at the thunder of your cataracts;
all your waves and your billows
  have gone over me.

By day the LORD commands his steadfast love,
and at night his song is with me,
a prayer to the God of my life.

I say to God, my rock,
'Why have you forgotten me?
Why must I walk about mournfully
because the enemy oppresses me?'
As with a deadly wound in my body,
my adversaries taunt me,
while they say to me continually,
'Where is your God?'

Why are you cast down, O my soul,
and why are you disquieted within me?
Hope in God; for I shall again praise him,
my help and my God.

Psalm 46

God is our refuge and strength,
a very present help in trouble.
Therefore we will not fear, though the earth should
change,
though the mountains shake in the heart of
the sea;
though its waters roar and foam,
though the mountains tremble with its tumult.

There is a river whose streams make glad the city
of God,
the holy habitation of the Most High.
God is in the midst of the city; it shall not be moved;
God will help it when the morning dawns.
The nations are in an uproar, the kingdoms totter;
he utters his voice, the earth melts.
The LORD of hosts is with us;
the God of Jacob is our refuge.

Come, behold the works of the LORD;
see what desolations he has brought on the earth.
He makes wars cease to the end of the earth;
he breaks the bow, and shatters the spear;
he burns the shields with fire.
'Be still, and know that I am God!
I am exalted among the nations,
I am exalted in the earth.'
The LORD of hosts is with us;
the God of Jacob is our refuge.

Psalm 90

LORD, you have been our dwelling-place
 in all generations.
Before the mountains were brought forth,
 or ever you had formed the earth and the world,
 from everlasting to everlasting you are God.

You turn us back to dust,
 and say, 'Turn back, you mortals.'
For a thousand years in your sight
 are like yesterday when it is past,
 or like a watch in the night.

You sweep them away; they are like a dream,
 like grass that is renewed in the morning;
in the morning it flourishes and is renewed;
 in the evening it fades and withers.

For we are consumed by your anger;
 by your wrath we are overwhelmed.
You have set our iniquities before you,
 our secret sins in the light of your countenance.

For all our days pass away under your wrath;
 our years come to an end like a sigh.
The days of our life are seventy years,
 or perhaps eighty, if we are strong;
even then their span is only toil and trouble;
 they are soon gone, and we fly away.

Who considers the power of your anger?
   Your wrath is as great as the fear that is due to you.
So teach us to count our days
   that we may gain a wise heart.

Turn, O LORD! How long?
   Have compassion on your servants!
Satisfy us in the morning with your steadfast love,
   so that we may rejoice and be glad all our days.
Make us glad for as many days as you have afflicted us,
   and for as many years as we have seen evil.
Let your work be manifest to your servants,
   and your glorious power to their children.
Let the favour of the Lord our God be upon us,
   and prosper for us the work of our hands –
      O prosper the work of our hands!

Psalm 91

You who live in the shelter of the Most High,
    who abide in the shadow of the Almighty,
will say to the LORD, 'My refuge and my fortress;
    my God, in whom I trust.'
For he will deliver you from the snare of the fowler
    and from the deadly pestilence;
he will cover you with his pinions,
    and under his wings you will find refuge;
    his faithfulness is a shield and buckler.
You will not fear the terror of the night,
    or the arrow that flies by day,
or the pestilence that stalks in darkness,
    or the destruction that wastes at noonday.

A thousand may fall at your side,
    ten thousand at your right hand,
    but it will not come near you.
You will only look with your eyes
    and see the punishment of the wicked.

Because you have made the LORD your refuge,
    the Most High your dwelling-place,
no evil shall befall you,
    no scourge come near your tent.

For he will command his angels concerning you
    to guard you in all your ways.
On their hands they will bear you up,
    so that you will not dash your foot against a stone.

You will tread on the lion and the adder,
   the young lion and the serpent you will trample
      under foot.

Those who love me, I will deliver;
   I will protect those who know my name.
When they call to me, I will answer them;
   I will be with them in trouble,
   I will rescue them and honour them.
With long life I will satisfy them,
   and show them my salvation.

Psalm 121

I lift up my eyes to the hills –
   from where will my help come?
My help comes from the LORD,
   who made heaven and earth.

He will not let your foot be moved;
   he who keeps you will not slumber.
He who keeps Israel
   will neither slumber nor sleep.

The LORD is your keeper;
   the LORD is your shade at your right hand.
The sun shall not strike you by day,
   nor the moon by night.

The LORD will keep you from all evil;
   he will keep your life.
The LORD will keep
   your going out and your coming in
   from this time on and for evermore.

Psalm 130

Out of the depths I cry to you, O LORD.
  Lord, hear my voice!
Let your ears be attentive
  to the voice of my supplications!

If you, O LORD, should mark iniquities,
  Lord, who could stand?
But there is forgiveness with you,
  so that you may be revered.

I wait for the LORD, my soul waits,
  and in his word I hope;
my soul waits for the Lord
  more than those who watch for the morning,
  more than those who watch for the morning.

O Israel, hope in the LORD!
  For with the LORD there is steadfast love,
  and with him is great power to redeem.
It is he who will redeem Israel
  from all its iniquities.

Psalm 139.1–18

O LORD, you have searched me and known me.
You know when I sit down and when I rise up;
    you discern my thoughts from far away.
You search out my path and my lying down,
    and are acquainted with all my ways.
Even before a word is on my tongue,
    O LORD, you know it completely.
You hem me in, behind and before,
    and lay your hand upon me.
Such knowledge is too wonderful for me;
    it is so high that I cannot attain it.

Where can I go from your spirit?
    Or where can I flee from your presence?
If I ascend to heaven, you are there;
    if I make my bed in Sheol, you are there.
If I take the wings of the morning
    and settle at the farthest limits of the sea,
even there your hand shall lead me,
    and your right hand shall hold me fast.
If I say, 'Surely the darkness shall cover me,
    and the light around me become night',
even the darkness is not dark to you;
    the night is as bright as the day,
    for darkness is as light to you.

For it was you who formed my inward parts;
  you knit me together in my mother's womb.
I praise you, for I am fearfully and wonderfully
    made.
  Wonderful are your works;
that I know very well.
  My frame was not hidden from you,
when I was being made in secret,
  intricately woven in the depths of the earth.
Your eyes beheld my unformed substance.
In your book were written
  all the days that were formed for me,
  when none of them as yet existed.
How weighty to me are your thoughts, O God!
  How vast is the sum of them!
I try to count them – they are more than the sand;
  I come to the end – I am still with you.

Ecclesiastes 3.1–15

For everything there is a season, and a time
    for every matter under heaven:
a time to be born, and a time to die;
a time to plant, and a time to pluck up what
    is planted;
a time to kill, and a time to heal;
a time to break down, and a time to build up;
a time to weep, and a time to laugh;
a time to mourn, and a time to dance;
a time to throw away stones, and a time to
    gather stones together;
a time to embrace, and a time to refrain from
    embracing;
a time to seek, and a time to lose;
a time to keep, and a time to throw away;
a time to tear, and a time to sew;
a time to keep silence, and a time to speak;
a time to love, and a time to hate;
a time for war, and a time for peace.

What gain have the workers from their toil? I have
seen the business that God has given to everyone
to be busy with. He has made everything suitable
for its time; moreover, he has put a sense of past
and future into their minds, yet they cannot find
out what God has done from the beginning to the
end. I know that there is nothing better for them
than to be happy and enjoy themselves as long as
they live; moreover, it is God's gift that all should

eat and drink and take pleasure in all their toil. I know that whatever God does endures for ever; nothing can be added to it, nor anything taken from it; God has done this, so that all should stand in awe before him. That which is, already has been; that which is to be, already is; and God seeks out what has gone by.

Song of Solomon 8.6–7

Set me as a seal upon your heart,
    as a seal upon your arm;
for love is strong as death,
    passion fierce as the grave.
Its flashes are flashes of fire,
    a raging flame.
Many waters cannot quench love,
    neither can floods drown it.
If one offered for love
    all the wealth of one's house,
    it would be utterly scorned.

Isaiah 35.1–10

The wilderness and the dry land shall be glad,
   the desert shall rejoice and blossom;
like the crocus it shall blossom abundantly,
   and rejoice with joy and singing.
The glory of Lebanon shall be given to it,
   the majesty of Carmel and Sharon.
They shall see the glory of the LORD,
   the majesty of our God.

Strengthen the weak hands,
   and make firm the feeble knees.
Say to those who are of a fearful heart,
   'Be strong, do not fear!
Here is your God.
   He will come with vengeance,
with terrible recompense.
   He will come and save you.'

Then the eyes of the blind shall be opened,
   and the ears of the deaf unstopped;
then the lame shall leap like a deer,
   and the tongue of the speechless sing for joy.
For waters shall break forth in the wilderness,
   and streams in the desert;
the burning sand shall become a pool,
   and the thirsty ground springs of water;
the haunt of jackals shall become a swamp,
   the grass shall become reeds and rushes.

A highway shall be there,
    and it shall be called the Holy Way;
the unclean shall not travel on it,
    but it shall be for God's people;
      no traveller, not even fools, shall go astray.
No lion shall be there,
    nor shall any ravenous beast come up on it;
they shall not be found there,
    but the redeemed shall walk there.
And the ransomed of the LORD shall return,
    and come to Zion with singing;
everlasting joy shall be upon their heads;
    they shall obtain joy and gladness,
    and sorrow and sighing shall flee away.

Isaiah 40.1–11

Comfort, O comfort my people,
  says your God.
Speak tenderly to Jerusalem,
  and cry to her
that she has served her term,
  that her penalty is paid,
that she has received from the LORD's hand
  double for all her sins.

A voice cries out:
'In the wilderness prepare the way of the LORD,
  make straight in the desert a highway for
    our God.
Every valley shall be lifted up,
  and every mountain and hill be made low;
the uneven ground shall become level,
  and the rough places a plain.
Then the glory of the LORD shall be revealed,
  and all people shall see it together,
  for the mouth of the LORD has spoken.'

A voice says, 'Cry out!'
  And I said, 'What shall I cry?'
All people are grass,
  their constancy is like the flower of the field.
The grass withers, the flower fades,
  when the breath of the LORD blows upon it;
  surely the people are grass.
The grass withers, the flower fades;
  but the word of our God will stand for ever.

Get you up to a high mountain,
  O Zion, herald of good tidings;
lift up your voice with strength,
  O Jerusalem, herald of good tidings,
  lift it up, do not fear;
say to the cities of Judah,
  'Here is your God!'
See, the Lord GOD comes with might,
  and his arm rules for him;
his reward is with him,
  and his recompense before him.
He will feed his flock like a shepherd;
  he will gather the lambs in his arms,
and carry them in his bosom,
  and gently lead the mother sheep.

Isaiah 40.28–31

Have you not known? Have you not heard?
The LORD is the everlasting God,
   the Creator of the ends of the earth.
He does not faint or grow weary;
   his understanding is unsearchable.
He gives power to the faint,
   and strengthens the powerless.
Even youths will faint and be weary,
   and the young will fall exhausted;
but those who wait for the LORD shall renew
     their strength,
   they shall mount up with wings like eagles,
they shall run and not be weary,
   they shall walk and not faint.

Lamentations 3.22-26

The steadfast love of the LORD never ceases,
 his mercies never come to an end;
they are new every morning;
 great is your faithfulness.
'The LORD is my portion,' says my soul,
 'therefore I will hope in him.'

The LORD is good to those who wait for him,
 to the soul that seeks him.
It is good that one should wait quietly
 for the salvation of the LORD.

Micah 6.6–8

'With what shall I come before the LORD,
   and bow myself before God on high?
Shall I come before him with burnt-offerings,
   with calves a year old?
Will the LORD be pleased with thousands of rams,
   with tens of thousands of rivers of oil?
Shall I give my firstborn for my transgression,
   the fruit of my body for the sin of my soul?'
He has told you, O mortal, what is good;
   and what does the LORD require of you
but to do justice, and to love kindness,
   and to walk humbly with your God?

Matthew 5.1–12

When Jesus saw the crowds, he went up the mountain; and after he sat down, his disciples came to him. Then he began to speak, and taught them, saying:

'Blessed are the poor in spirit, for theirs is the kingdom of heaven.

'Blessed are those who mourn, for they will be comforted.

'Blessed are the meek, for they will inherit the earth.

'Blessed are those who hunger and thirst for righteousness, for they will be filled.

'Blessed are the merciful, for they will receive mercy.

'Blessed are the pure in heart, for they will see God.

'Blessed are the peacemakers, for they will be called children of God.

'Blessed are those who are persecuted for righteousness' sake, for theirs is the kingdom of heaven.

'Blessed are you when people revile you and persecute you and utter all kinds of evil against you falsely on my account. Rejoice and be glad, for your reward is great in heaven, for in the same way they persecuted the prophets who were before you.

Mark 10.13-16

People were bringing little children to him in order that he might touch them; and the disciples spoke sternly to them. But when Jesus saw this, he was indignant and said to them, 'Let the little children come to me; do not stop them; for it is to such as these that the kingdom of God belongs. Truly I tell you, whoever does not receive the kingdom of God as a little child will never enter it.' And he took them up in his arms, laid his hands on them, and blessed them.

Luke 2.29-32

'Master, now you are dismissing your servant
    in peace,
  according to your word;
for my eyes have seen your salvation,
  which you have prepared in the presence
    of all peoples,
a light for revelation to the Gentiles
  and for glory to your people Israel.'

Luke 24.1–12

But on the first day of the week, at early dawn, they came to the tomb, taking the spices that they had prepared. They found the stone rolled away from the tomb, but when they went in, they did not find the body. While they were perplexed about this, suddenly two men in dazzling clothes stood beside them. The women were terrified and bowed their faces to the ground, but the men said to them, 'Why do you look for the living among the dead? He is not here, but has risen. Remember how he told you, while he was still in Galilee, that the Son of Man must be handed over to sinners, and be crucified, and on the third day rise again.' Then they remembered his words, and returning from the tomb, they told all this to the eleven and to all the rest. Now it was Mary Magdalene, Joanna, Mary the mother of James, and the other women with them who told this to the apostles. But these words seemed to them an idle tale, and they did not believe them. But Peter got up and ran to the tomb; stooping and looking in, he saw the linen cloths by themselves; then he went home, amazed at what had happened.

John 10.27-29

My sheep hear my voice. I know them, and they
follow me. I give them eternal life, and they will
never perish. No one will snatch them out of my
hand. What my Father has given me is greater than
all else, and no one can snatch it out of the Father's
hand.'

John 11.20–26

When Martha heard that Jesus was coming, she went and met him, while Mary stayed at home. Martha said to Jesus, 'Lord, if you had been here, my brother would not have died. But even now I know that God will give you whatever you ask of him.' Jesus said to her, 'Your brother will rise again.' Martha said to him, 'I know that he will rise again in the resurrection on the last day.' Jesus said to her, 'I am the resurrection and the life. Those who believe in me, even though they die, will live, and everyone who lives and believes in me will never die.'

John 14.1-7

'Do not let your hearts be troubled. Believe in God, believe also in me. In my Father's house there are many dwelling-places. If it were not so, would I have told you that I go to prepare a place for you? And if I go and prepare a place for you, I will come again and will take you to myself, so that where I am, there you may be also. And you know the way to the place where I am going.' Thomas said to him, 'Lord, we do not know where you are going. How can we know the way?' Jesus said to him, 'I am the way, and the truth, and the life. No one comes to the Father except through me. If you know me, you will know my Father also. From now on you do know him and have seen him.'

John 14.15–20

'If you love me, you will keep my commandments. And I will ask the Father, and he will give you another Advocate, to be with you for ever. This is the Spirit of truth, whom the world cannot receive, because it neither sees him nor knows him. You know him, because he abides with you, and he will be in you.

'I will not leave you orphaned; I am coming to you. In a little while the world will no longer see me, but you will see me; because I live, you also will live. On that day you will know that I am in my Father, and you in me, and I in you.'

John 20.1–18

Early on the first day of the week, while it was still dark, Mary Magdalene came to the tomb and saw that the stone had been removed from the tomb. So she ran and went to Simon Peter and the other disciple, the one whom Jesus loved, and said to them, 'They have taken the Lord out of the tomb, and we do not know where they have laid him.' Then Peter and the other disciple set out and went towards the tomb. The two were running together, but the other disciple outran Peter and reached the tomb first. He bent down to look in and saw the linen wrappings lying there, but he did not go in. Then Simon Peter came, following him, and went into the tomb. He saw the linen wrappings lying there, and the cloth that had been on Jesus' head, not lying with the linen wrappings but rolled up in a place by itself. Then the other disciple, who reached the tomb first, also went in, and he saw and believed; for as yet they did not understand the scripture, that he must rise from the dead. Then the disciples returned to their homes.

But Mary stood weeping outside the tomb. As she wept, she bent over to look into the tomb; and she saw two angels in white, sitting where the body of Jesus had been lying, one at the head and the other at the feet. They said to her, 'Woman, why are you weeping?' She said to them, 'They have taken away my Lord, and I do not know where they have laid him.' When she had said this, she turned round and saw Jesus standing there, but she did not know that it was Jesus. Jesus said to her, 'Woman, why are you weeping? For whom are you looking?' Supposing him to be the gardener, she said to him, 'Sir, if you have carried him away, tell me where you have laid him, and I will take him away.' Jesus said to her, 'Mary!' She turned and said to him in Hebrew, 'Rabbouni!' (which means Teacher). Jesus said to her, 'Do not hold on to me, because I have not yet ascended to the Father. But go to my brothers and say to them, "I am ascending to my Father and your Father, to my God and your God."' Mary Magdalene went and announced to the disciples, 'I have seen the Lord'; and she told them that he had said these things to her.

Romans 8.35–39

Who will separate us from the love of Christ? Will hardship, or distress, or persecution, or famine, or nakedness, or peril, or sword? As it is written,

> 'For your sake we are being killed all day long; we are accounted as sheep to be slaughtered.'

No, in all these things we are more than conquerors through him who loved us. For I am convinced that neither death, nor life, nor angels, nor rulers, nor things present, nor things to come, nor powers, nor height, nor depth, nor anything else in all creation, will be able to separate us from the love of God in Christ Jesus our Lord.

1 Corinthians 13.1–13

If I speak in the tongues of mortals and of angels, but do not have love, I am a noisy gong or a clanging cymbal. And if I have prophetic powers, and understand all mysteries and all knowledge, and if I have all faith, so as to remove mountains, but do not have love, I am nothing. If I give away all my possessions, and if I hand over my body so that I may boast, but do not have love, I gain nothing. Love is patient; love is kind; love is not envious or boastful or arrogant or rude. It does not insist on its own way; it is not irritable or resentful; it does not rejoice in wrongdoing, but rejoices in the truth. It bears all things, believes all things, hopes all things, endures all things. Love never ends. But as for prophecies, they will come to an end; as for tongues, they will cease; as for knowledge, it will come to an end. For we know only in part, and we prophesy only in part; but when the complete comes, the partial will come to an end. When I was a child, I spoke like a child, I thought like a child, I reasoned like a child; when I became an adult, I put an end to childish ways. For now we see in a mirror, dimly, but then we will see face to face. Now I know only in part; then I will know fully, even as I have been fully known. And now faith, hope, and love abide, these three; and the greatest of these is love.

1 Corinthians 15.12-22

Now if Christ is proclaimed as raised from the dead, how can some of you say there is no resurrection of the dead? If there is no resurrection of the dead, then Christ has not been raised; and if Christ has not been raised, then our proclamation has been in vain and your faith has been in vain. We are even found to be misrepresenting God, because we testified of God that he raised Christ – whom he did not raise if it is true that the dead are not raised. For if the dead are not raised, then Christ has not been raised. If Christ has not been raised, your faith is futile and you are still in your sins. Then those also who have died in Christ have perished. If for this life only we have hoped in Christ, we are of all people most to be pitied.

But in fact Christ has been raised from the dead, the first fruits of those who have died. For since death came through a human being, the resurrection of the dead has also come through a human being; for as all die in Adam, so all will be made alive in Christ.

1 Corinthians 15.35-49

But someone will ask, 'How are the dead raised? With what kind of body do they come?' Fool! What you sow does not come to life unless it dies. And as for what you sow, you do not sow the body that is to be, but a bare seed, perhaps of wheat or of some other grain. But God gives it a body as he has chosen, and to each kind of seed its own body. Not all flesh is alike, but there is one flesh for human beings, another for animals, another for birds, and another for fish. There are both heavenly bodies and earthly bodies, but the glory of the heavenly is one thing, and that of the earthly is another. There is one glory of the sun, and another glory of the moon, and another glory of the stars; indeed, star differs from star in glory.

So it is with the resurrection of the dead. What is sown is perishable, what is raised is imperishable. It is sown in dishonour, it is raised in glory. It is sown in weakness, it is raised in power. It is sown a physical body, it is raised a spiritual body. If there is a physical body, there is also a spiritual body. Thus it is written, 'The first man, Adam, became a living being'; the last Adam became a life-giving spirit. But it is not the spiritual that is first, but the physical, and then the spiritual. The first man was from the earth, a man of dust; the second man is from heaven. As was the man of dust, so are those who are of the dust; and as is the man of heaven, so are those who are of heaven. Just as we have borne the image of the man of dust, we will also bear the image of the man of heaven.

1 Corinthians 15.51–55

Listen, I will tell you a mystery! We will not all die, but we will all be changed, in a moment, in the twinkling of an eye, at the last trumpet. For the trumpet will sound, and the dead will be raised imperishable, and we will be changed. For this perishable body must put on imperishability, and this mortal body must put on immortality. When this perishable body puts on imperishability, and this mortal body puts on immortality, then the saying that is written will be fulfilled:

'Death has been swallowed up in victory.'
'Where, O death, is your victory?
    Where, O death, is your sting?'

2 Corinthians 1.3–7

Blessed be the God and Father of our Lord Jesus
Christ, the Father of mercies and the God of all
consolation, who consoles us in all our affliction,
so that we may be able to console those who are
in any affliction with the consolation with which
we ourselves are consoled by God. For just as the
sufferings of Christ are abundant for us, so also
our consolation is abundant through Christ. If
we are being afflicted, it is for your consolation
and salvation; if we are being consoled, it is for
your consolation, which you experience when you
patiently endure the same sufferings that we are
also suffering. Our hope for you is unshaken; for
we know that as you share in our sufferings, so
also you share in our consolation.

Colossians 3.12-15

As God's chosen ones, holy and beloved, clothe yourselves with compassion, kindness, humility, meekness, and patience. Bear with one another and, if anyone has a complaint against another, forgive each other; just as the Lord has forgiven you, so you also must forgive. Above all, clothe yourselves with love, which binds everything together in perfect harmony. And let the peace of Christ rule in your hearts, to which indeed you were called in the one body. And be thankful.

2 Timothy 4.6–8

As for me, I am already being poured out as a libation, and the time of my departure has come. I have fought the good fight, I have finished the race, I have kept the faith. From now on there is reserved for me the crown of righteousness, which the Lord, the righteous judge, will give me on that day, and not only to me but also to all who have longed for his appearing.

1 Peter 1.3-9

Blessed be the God and Father of our Lord Jesus Christ! By his great mercy he has given us a new birth into a living hope through the resurrection of Jesus Christ from the dead, and into an inheritance that is imperishable, undefiled, and unfading, kept in heaven for you, who are being protected by the power of God through faith for a salvation ready to be revealed in the last time. In this you rejoice, even if now for a little while you have had to suffer various trials, so that the genuineness of your faith – being more precious than gold that, though perishable, is tested by fire – may be found to result in praise and glory and honour when Jesus Christ is revealed. Although you have not seen him, you love him; and even though you do not see him now, you believe in him and rejoice with an indescribable and glorious joy, for you are receiving the outcome of your faith, the salvation of your souls.

Revelation 21.1-7

Then I saw a new heaven and a new earth; for the first heaven and the first earth had passed away, and the sea was no more. And I saw the holy city, the new Jerusalem, coming down out of heaven from God, prepared as a bride adorned for her husband. And I heard a loud voice from the throne saying,

'See, the home of God is among mortals.
He will dwell with them;
they will be his peoples,
and God himself will be with them;
he will wipe every tear from their eyes.
Death will be no more;
mourning and crying and pain will be no more,
for the first things have passed away.'

And the one who was seated on the throne said, 'See, I am making all things new.' Also he said, 'Write this, for these words are trustworthy and true.' Then he said to me, 'It is done! I am the Alpha and the Omega, the beginning and the end. To the thirsty I will give water as a gift from the spring of the water of life. Those who conquer will inherit these things, and I will be their God and they will be my children.'

Poems and reflections

When

Sophia de Mello Breyner Andresen

When my body falls sick and I die
The garden will still be here, the sea and the sky,
And the four seasons, just as they do today,
Will dance at my door.

In April, others will stroll in the orchard
Where I so often walked.
There will be long sunsets over the sea,
Others will love the things I loved.

The same glow, the same celebration,
The same garden at my door,
The same golden-haired forest,
Just as if I hadn't died.

(Translated from the Portuguese
by Margaret Jull Costa)

A Celtic blessing

Anonymous

Deep peace of the running wave to you,
Deep peace of the flowing air to you,
Deep peace of the quiet earth to you,
Deep peace of the shining stars to you,
Deep peace of the Son of Peace to you.
May the road rise to meet you;
May the wind be always at your back;
May the sun shine warm upon your face;
May the rains fall softly upon your fields.
Until we meet again,
May God hold you in the hollow of His hand.

How long will the pain last?

Anonymous

'How long will the pain last?' a broken-hearted mourner asked me. 'All the rest of your Life.'

I have to answer truthfully. We never quite forget.

No matter how many years pass, we remember.

The loss of a loved one is like a major operation.

Part of us is removed, and we have a scar for the rest of our lives.

As years go by, we manage.

There are things to do, people to care for, tasks that call for full attention.

But the pain is still there, not far below the surface.

We see a face that looks familiar, hear a voice that echoes, see a photograph in someone's album, see a landscape that once we saw together, and it seems as though a knife were in the wound again.

But not so painfully.

And mixed with joy, too.

Because remembering a happy time is not all sorrow, it brings happiness with it.

How long will the pain last?

All the rest of your life.

But the thing to remember is that not only the pain will last, but the blessed memories as well.

Tears are proof of life.
The more love, the more tears.
If this be true, then how could we ever ask that the pain cease altogether?
For then the memory of love would go with it.
The pain of grief is the price we pay for love.

'Not, how did he die, but how did he live?'
Anonymous

Not, how did he die, but how did he live?
Not, what did he gain, but what did he give?
These are the units to measure the worth
Of a man as a man, regardless of birth.
Not what was his church, nor what was his creed?
But had he befriended those really in need?
Was he ever ready, with word of good cheer,
To bring back a smile, to banish a tear?
Not what did the sketch in the newspaper say,
But how many were sorry when he passed away?

Weep you no more, sad fountains

Anonymous

Weep you no more, sad fountains;
  What need you flow so fast?
Look how the snowy mountains
  Heaven's sun doth gently waste.
  But my sun's heavenly eyes
    View not your weeping,
    That now lie sleeping
  Softly, now softly lies
    Sleeping.

Sleep is a reconciling,
  A rest that peace begets.
Doth not the sun rise smiling
  When fair at even he sets?
  Rest you then, rest, sad eyes,
    Melt not in weeping
    While she lies sleeping
  Softly, now softly lies
    Sleeping.

After I have gone
Vera I. Arlett

Speak my name softly after I have gone.
I loved the quiet things, the flowers and the dew,
Field mice; birds homing; and the frost that shone
On nursery windows when my years were few;
And autumn mists subduing hill and plain
and blurring outlines of those older moods
that follow, after loss and grief and pain –
And last and best, a gentle laugh with friends,
All bitterness foregone, and evening near.
If we be kind and faithful when day ends,
We shall not meet that ragged starveling 'fear'
As one by one we take the unknown way –
Speak my name softly – there's no more to say –

I thought I'd write my own obituary
Simon Armitage

I thought I'd write my own obituary. Instead,
I wrote the poem for when I'm risen from the dead:

Ignite the flares, connect the phones, wind all the
    clocks;
the sun goes rusty like a medal in its box –
collect it from the loft. Peg out the stars,
replace the bulbs of Jupiter and Mars.
A man like that takes something with him when he dies,
but he has wept the coins that rested on his eyes,
eased out the stopper from the mouthpiece of the cave,
exhumed his own white body from the grave.

Unlock the rivers, hoist the dawn and launch the sea.
Set up the skittles of the orchard and the wood again,
now everything is clear and straight and free and good
    again.

Funeral blues

W. H. Auden

Stop all the clocks, cut off the telephone,
Prevent the dog from barking with a juicy bone,
Silence the pianos and with muffled drum
Bring out the coffin, let the mourners come.

Let aeroplanes circle moaning overhead
Scribbling on the sky the message He Is Dead,
Put crêpe bows round the white necks of the public
doves,
Let the traffic policemen wear black cotton gloves.

He was my North, my South, my East and West,
My working week and my Sunday rest,
My noon, my midnight, my talk, my song;
I thought that love would last for ever: I was wrong.

The stars are not wanted now: put out every one;
Pack up the moon and dismantle the sun;
Pour away the ocean and sweep up the wood;
For nothing now can ever come to any good.

If I could tell you

W. H. Auden

Time will say nothing but I told you so,
Time only knows the price we have to pay;
If I could tell you I would let you know.

If we should weep when clowns put on their show,
If we should stumble when musicians play,
Time will say nothing but I told you so.

There are no fortunes to be told, although,
Because I love you more than I can say,
If I could tell you I would let you know.

The winds must come from somewhere when they
    blow,
There must be reasons why the leaves decay;
Time will say nothing but I told you so.

Perhaps the roses really want to grow,
The vision seriously intends to stay;
If I could tell you I would let you know.

Suppose the lions all get up and go,
And the brooks and soldiers run away;
Will Time say nothing but I told you so?
If I could tell you I would let you know.

From *The Gift of Peace*
Cardinal Joseph Bernardin

As I write these final words, my heart is filled with joy. I am at peace.

It is the first day of November, and fall is giving way to winter. Soon the trees will lose the vibrant colours of their leaves and snow will cover the ground. The earth will shut down, and people will race to and from their destinations bundled up for warmth. Chicago winters are harsh. It is a time of dying.

But we know that spring will soon come with all its new life and wonder . . .

Many people have asked me to tell them about heaven and the afterlife. I sometimes smile at the request because I do not know any more than they do. Yet, when one young man asked if I looked forward to being united with God and all those who have gone before me, I made a connection to something I said earlier in this book. The first time I travelled with my mother and sister to my parents' homeland of Tonadico di Primiero, in northern Italy, I felt as if I had been there before. After years of looking through my mother's photo albums, I knew the mountains, the land, the houses, the people. As soon as we entered the valley, I said, 'My God, I know this place. I am home.' Somehow I think crossing from this life into life eternal will be similar. I will be home.

The peace of wild things
Wendell Berry

When despair for the world grows in me
and I wake in the night at the least sound
in fear of what my life and my children's lives
   may be,
I go and lie down where the wood drake
rests in his beauty on the water, and the great
   heron feeds.
I come into the peace of wild things
who do not tax their lives with forethought
of grief. I come into the presence of still water.
And I feel above me the day-blind stars
waiting with their light. For a time
I rest in the grace of the world, and am free.

From *Letters and Papers from Prison*
Dietrich Bonhoeffer

Nothing can make up for the absence of someone whom we love, and it would be wrong to try to find a substitute; we must simply hold out and see it through. That sounds very hard at first, but at the same time it is a great consolation, for the gap, as long as it remains unfilled, preserves the bonds between us. It is nonsense to say that God fills the gap; God doesn't fill it, but on the contrary, keeps it empty and so helps us to keep alive our former communion with each other, even at the cost of pain.

What is Dying?

Attributed to Charles Henry Brent

I am standing upon the seashore. A ship at my side spreads her white sails to the morning breeze and starts for the blue ocean. She is an object of beauty and strength, and I stand and watch her until at length she hangs like a speck of white cloud just where the sea and sky come down to meet and mingle with each other. Then some one at my side says, 'There! She's gone!' Gone where? Gone from my sight, that is all. She is just as large in the mast and hull and spar as she was when she left my side, and just as able to bear her load of living freight to the place of her destination. Her diminished size is in me, and not in her. And just at that moment, when someone at my side says, 'There! She's gone!' there are other eyes that are watching for her coming and other voices ready to take up the glad shout, 'There she comes!' And that is – dying.

No coward soul is mine
Emily Brontë

No coward soul is mine
No trembler in the world's storm-troubled sphere
I see Heaven's glories shine
And Faith shines equal arming me from Fear

O God within my breast
Almighty ever-present Deity
Life, that in me hast rest
As I Undying Life, have power in thee

Vain are the thousand creeds
That move men's hearts, unutterably vain,
Worthless as withered weeds
Or idlest froth amid the boundless main

To waken doubt in one
Holding so fast by thy infinity
So surely anchored on
The steadfast rock of Immortality

With wide-embracing love
Thy spirit animates eternal years
Pervades and broods above,
Changes, sustains, dissolves, creates and rears

Though Earth and moon were gone
And suns and universes ceased to be
And thou wert left alone
Every Existence would exist in thee

There is not room for Death
Nor atom that his might could render void
Since thou art Being and Breath
And what thou art may never be destroyed

Elegy

George Mackay Brown

That one should leave the greenwood suddenly
In the good comrade-time of youth,
And clothed in the first coat of truth
Set out on an uncharted sea.

Who'll ever know what star
Summoned him, what mysterious shell
Locked in his ear that music and that spell,
And what grave ship was waiting for him there?

The greenwood empties soon of leaf and song.
Truth turns to pain. Our coats grow sere.
Barren the comings and goings on this shore.
He anchors off the Island of the Young.

Sonnet 43 from Sonnets from the Portuguese

Elizabeth Barrett Browning

How do I love thee? Let me count the ways.
I love thee to the depth and breadth and height
My soul can reach, when feeling out of sight
For the ends of Being and ideal Grace.
I love thee to the level of everyday's
Most quiet need, by sun and candlelight.
I love thee freely, as men strive for Right;
I love thee purely, as they turn from Praise.
I love thee with the passion put to use
In my old griefs, and with my childhood's faith.
I love thee with a love I seemed to lose
With my lost saints, I love thee with the breath,
Smiles, tears, of all my life! and, if God choose,
I shall but love thee better after death.

From *The Pilgrim's Progress*
John Bunyan

I see myself now at the end of my journey; my toilsome days are ended. I am going now to see that head which was crowned with thorns, and that face which was spit upon for me. I have formerly lived by hearsay and faith, but now I go where I shall live by sight, and shall be with Him in whose company I delight myself. I have loved to hear my Lord spoken of; and wherever I have seen the print of his shoe in the earth, there I have coveted to set my foot too. His name to me has been as a civet-box; yea, sweeter than all perfumes. His voice to me has been most sweet; and his countenance I have more desired than they that have most desired the light of the sun. His word I did use to gather for my food, and for antidotes against my faintings. He has held me, and has kept me from mine iniquities; yea, my steps hath he strengthened in his way.

Now, while he was thus in discourse, his countenance changed; his strong man bowed under him; and after he had said, 'Take me, for I come unto Thee!' he ceased to be seen of them.

But glorious it was to see how the open region was filled with horses and chariots, with trumpeters and pipers, with singers and players on stringed instruments, to welcome the pilgrims as they went up, and followed one another in at the beautiful gate of the city.

From *The Pilgrim's Progress*
John Bunyan

After this it was noised abroad that Mr Valiant-for-Truth was taken with a summons by the same post as the other; and had this for a token that the summons was true, that his pitcher was broken at the fountain.

When he understood it, he called for his friends, and told them of it. Then said he, 'I am going to my Father's; and though with great difficulty I am got hither, yet now I do not repent me of all the trouble I have been at to arrive where I am.

My sword I give to him that shall succeed me in my pilgrimage; and my courage and skill to him that can get it. My marks and scars I carry with me, to be a witness for me that I have fought his battles who now will be my Rewarder.

When the day that he must go hence was come, many accompanied him to the riverside; into which as he went he said, 'Death, where is thy sting?' And as he went down deeper, he said, 'Grave, where is thy victory?' So he passed over; and all the trumpets sounded for him on the other side.

Epitaph on a friend
Robert Burns

An honest man here lies at rest,
The friend of man, the friend of truth,
The friend of age, and guide of youth:
Few hearts like his, with virtue warm'd,
Few heads with knowledge so inform'd:
If there's another world, he lives in bliss;
If there is none, he made the best of this.

A song of living

Amelia Josephine Burr

Because I have loved life, I shall have no sorrow to die.
I have sent up my gladness on wings, to be lost in the
blue of the sky.
I have run and leaped with the rain, I have taken the
wind to my breast.
My cheek like a drowsy child to the face of the earth I
have pressed.
Because I have loved life, I shall have no sorrow to die.
I have kissed young Love on the lips, I have heard his
song to the end.
I have struck my hand like a seal in the loyal hand of
a friend.
I have known the peace of heaven, the comfort of
work done well.
I have longed for death in the darkness and risen alive
out of hell.
Because I have loved life, I shall have no sorrow to die.
I give a share of my soul to the world where my course
is run.
I know that another shall finish the task I must leave
undone.
I know that no flower, no flint was in vain on the
path I trod.
As one looks on a face through a window, through life
I have looked on God.
Because I have loved life, I shall have no sorrow to die.

We must not weep at an end
David Burrows

We must not weep at an end
For there is no end.
We are not what we were.
We cannot lose what we have gained.
We have met, we have touched each other
   with smiles,
Exchanged unknown emotions.
We have embraced without shame.
We have met for a reason,
A brief interlude in time,
And so we part, the purpose done.

We'll go no more a-roving
Lord Byron

So, we'll go no more a-roving
So late into the night,
Though the heart be still as loving,
And the moon be still as bright.

For the sword outwears its sheath,
And the soul wears out the breast,
And the heart must pause to breathe,
And Love itself have rest.

Though the night was made for loving,
And the day returns too soon,
Yet we'll go no more a-roving
By the light of the moon.

Late fragment

Raymond Carver

And did you get what
you wanted from this life, even so?
I did.
And what did you want?
To call myself beloved, to feel myself
beloved on the earth.

The dead
Billy Collins

The dead are always looking down on us, they say,
while we are putting on our shoes or making a sandwich,
they are looking down through the glass-bottom boats
    of heaven
as they row themselves slowly through eternity.

They watch the tops of our heads moving below on earth,
and when we lie down in a field or on a couch,
drugged perhaps by the hum of a warm afternoon,
they think we are looking back at them,

which makes them lift their oars and fall silent
and wait, like parents, for us to close our eyes.

My *funeral*
Wendy Cope

I hope I can trust you, friends, not to use our relationship
As an excuse for an unsolicited ego-trip.
I have seen enough of them at funerals and they make
   me cross.
At this one, though deceased, I aim to be the boss.
If you are asked to talk about me for five minutes,
   please do not go on for eight.
There is a strict timetable at the crematorium and
   nobody wants to be late.
If invited to read a poem, just read the bloody poem.
   If requested
To sing a song, just sing it, as suggested,
And don't say anything. Though I will not be there,
Glancing pointedly at my watch and fixing the speaker
   with a malevolent stare,
Remember that this was how I always reacted
When I felt that anybody's speech, sermon or poetry
   reading was becoming too protracted.
Yes, I was impatient and intolerant, and not always
   polite.
And if there aren't many people at my funeral, it will
   serve me right.

I'm here for a short visit only
Noël Coward

I'm here for a short visit only,
And I'd rather be loved than hated.
Eternity may be lonely
When my body's disintegrated;
And that which is loosely termed my soul
Goes whizzing off through the infinite
By means of some vague remote control.
I'd like to think I was missed a bit.

She died,—this was the way she died
Emily Dickinson

She died,—this was the way she died;
And when her breath was done,
Took up her simple wardrobe
And started for the sun.

Her little figure at the gate
The angels must have spied,
Since I could never find her
Upon the mortal side.

After great pain a formal feeling comes
Emily Dickinson

After great pain a formal feeling comes –
The nerves sit ceremonious like tombs;
The stiff Heart questions – was it He that bore?
And yesterday – or centuries before?

The feet mechanical
Go round a wooden way
Of ground or air or Ought, regardless grown,
A quartz contentment like a stone.

This is the hour of lead
Remembered if outlived,
As freezing persons recollect the snow –
First chill, then stupor, then the letting go.

If I can stop one heart from breaking
Emily Dickinson

If I can stop one heart from breaking,
I shall not live in vain:
If I can ease one life the aching,
Or cool one pain,
Or help one fainting robin
Unto his nest again,
I shall not live in vain.

Holy Sonnet X

John Donne

Death be not proud, though some have called thee
Mighty and dreadful, for thou art not so,
For, those, whom thou think'st thou dost overthrow,
Die not, poor death, nor yet canst thou kill me.
From rest and sleep, which but thy pictures be,
Much pleasure, then from thee, much more must flow,
And soonest our best men with thee do go,
Rest of their bones, and soul's delivery.
Thou art slave to Fate, chance, kings, and desperate men,
And dost with poison, war, and sickness dwell,
And poppy, or charms can make us sleep as well,
And better than thy stroke; why swell'st thou then?
One short sleep past, we wake eternally,
And death shall be no more; death, thou shalt die.

After a sermon by John Donne

Bring us, O Lord God, at our last awakening into
the house and gate of heaven; to enter into that
gate and dwell in that house, where there shall be
no darkness nor dazzling, but one equal light; no
noise nor silence, but one equal music; no fears
nor hopes, but one equal possession; no ends, nor
beginnings, but one equal eternity; in the habita-
tions of thy glory and dominion, world without
end. Amen.

Sandra's mobile
Douglas Dunn

A constant artist, dedicated to
Curves, shapes, the pleasant shades, the feel of colour,
She did not care what shapes, what red, what blue,
Scorning the dull to ridicule the duller
With a disinterested, loyal eye.
So Sandra brought her this and taped it up –
Three seagulls from a white and indoor sky –
A gift of old artistic comradeship.
'Blow on them, Love.' Those silent birds winged round
On thermals of my breath. On her last night,
Trying to stay awake, I saw love crowned
In tears and wooden birds and candlelight.
She did not wake again. To prove our love
Each gull, each gull, each gull, turned into a dove.

Attempts at the rational approach
Edna Eglinton

It isn't in important situations
that I miss you.
There is always someone who will help
when the toilet floods
or the tiles blow down.
I've learnt to wire a plug,
put up a shelf, to improvise,
make do, or go without.

I have grown a hardened shell
to wear when walking on my own
into restaurants, theatres,
cinemas and bars.

I have grown accustomed
to causing an odd number,
being partnerless at parties,
disturbing symmetry.

Till suddenly I hear the name
of a place we used to visit –
see a snippet in the paper
about an old-time friend –
think up a silly pun
which you would understand . . .

I have learned new thoughts,
new skills, tested new ventures,
found diversion in a dozen
first-time ways . . .

But when the car-keys disappear
from where I left them,
when next-door's prowling cat
finds an open window,
when the sugarbowl slides off
the kitchen table –
there is no one here to shout at
but myself.

From *East Coker*
T. S. Eliot

Home is where one starts from. As we grow older
The world becomes stranger, the pattern more
   complicated
Of dead and living. Not the intense moment
Isolated, with no before and after,
But a lifetime burning in every moment
And not the lifetime of one man only
But of old stones that cannot be deciphered.
There is a time for the evening under starlight,
A time for the evening under lamplight
(The evening with the photograph album).
Love is most nearly itself
When here and now cease to matter.
Old men ought to be explorers
Here or there does not matter
We must be still and still moving
Into another intensity
For a further union, a deeper communion
Through the dark cold and the empty desolation,
The wave cry, the wind cry, the vast waters
Of the petrel and the porpoise. In my end is my
   beginning.

The ideal

James Fenton

This is where I came from.
I passed this way.
This should not be shameful
Or hard to say.

A self is a self.
It is not a screen.
A person should respect
What he has been.

This is my past
Which I shall not discard.
This is the ideal.
This is hard.

Nothing gold can stay
Robert Frost

Nature's first green is gold,
Her hardest hue to hold.
Her early leaf's a flower;
But only so an hour.
Then leaf subsides to leaf.
So Eden sank to grief,
So dawn goes down to day.
Nothing gold can stay.

Yes

Tess Gallagher

Now we are like that flat cone of sand
in the garden of the Silver Pavilion in Kyoto
designed to appear only in moonlight.

Do you want me to mourn?
Do you want me to wear black?

Or like moonlight on whitest sand
to use your dark, to gleam, to shimmer?

I gleam. I mourn.

On *death* from *The Prophet*
Kahlil Gibran

You would know the secret of death.

But how shall you find it unless you seek it in the heart of life?

The owl whose night-bound eyes are blind unto the day cannot unveil the mystery of light.

If you would indeed behold the spirit of death, open your heart wide unto the body of life.

For life and death are one, even as the river and the sea are one.

In the depth of your hopes and desires lies your silent knowledge of the beyond;

And like seeds dreaming beneath the snow your heart dreams of spring.

Trust the dreams, for in them is hidden the gate to eternity.

Your fear of death is but the trembling of the shepherd when he stands before the king whose hand is to be laid upon him in honour.

Is the shepherd not joyful beneath his trembling, that he shall wear the mark of the king?

Yet is he not more mindful of his trembling?

For what is it to die but to stand naked in the wind and to melt into the sun?

And what is it to cease breathing but to free the breath from its restless tides, that it may rise and expand and seek God unencumbered?

Only when you drink from the river of silence shall you indeed sing.

And when you have reached the mountain top, then you shall begin to climb.

And when the earth shall claim your limbs, then shall you truly dance.

From *Joyce By Herself and Her Friends*
Joyce Grenfell

If I should go before the rest of you
Break not a flower nor inscribe a stone,
Nor when I'm gone speak in a Sunday voice
But be the usual selves that I have known.
        Weep if you must,
        Parting is hell,
But life goes on,
So sing as well.

Turn again

Mary Lee Hall

If I should die and leave you here awhile,
Be not like others, sore undone, who keep
Long vigils by the silent dust, and weep.
For my sake, turn again to life and smile,
Nerving thy heart and trembling hand to do
Something to comfort weaker hearts than thine.
Complete those dear unfinished tasks of mine,
And I perchance may therein comfort you!

Afterwards
Thomas Hardy

When the Present has latched its postern behind my
    tremulous stay,
  And the May month flaps its glad green leaves like
    wings,
Delicate-filmed as new-spun silk, will the neighbours say,
  'He was a man who used to notice such things'?

If it be in the dusk when, like an eyelid's soundless blink,
  The dewfall-hawk comes crossing the shades to alight
Upon the wind-warped upland thorn, a gazer may think,
  'To him this must have been a familiar sight.'

If I pass during some nocturnal blackness, mothy and warm,
  When the hedgehog travels furtively over the lawn,
One may say, 'He strove that such innocent creatures
    should come to no harm,
  But he could do little for them; and now he is gone.'

If, when hearing that I have been stilled at last, they
    stand at the door,
  Watching the full-starred heavens that winter sees,
Will this thought rise on those who will meet my face
    no more,
  'He was one who had an eye for such mysteries'?

And will any say when my bell of quittance is heard in
    the gloom,
  And a crossing breeze cuts a pause in its outrollings,
Till they rise again, as they were a new bell's boom,
  'He hears it not now, but used to notice such things'?

The walk

Thomas Hardy

You did not walk with me
      Of late to the hill-top tree
         By the gated ways,
         As in earlier days;
         You were weak and lame,
         So you never came,
And I went alone, and I did not mind,
Not thinking of you as left behind.

      I walked up there to-day
      Just in the former way;
         Surveyed around
         The familiar ground
         By myself again:
         What difference, then?
Only that underlying sense
Of the look of a room on returning thence.

Remember me
David Harkins

You can shed tears that she is gone
Or you can smile because she has lived.

You can close your eyes and pray that she will come back
Or you can open your eyes and see all that she has left.

Your heart can be empty because you can't see her
Or you can be full of the love that you shared.

You can turn your back on tomorrow and live yesterday
Or you can be happy for tomorrow because of yesterday.

You can remember her and only that she is gone
Or you can cherish her memory and let it live on.

You can cry and close your mind, be empty and turn
    your back
Or you can do what she would want: smile, open
    your eyes,
love and go on.

A thousand years, you said

Lady Heguri

A thousand years, you said
As our two hearts melted.
I look at the hand you held
And the ache is too hard to bear.

Love (III)

George Herbert

Love bade me welcome: yet my soul drew back,
    Guiltie of dust and sinne.
But quick-ey'd Love, observing me grow slack
    From my first entrance in,
Drew nearer to me, sweetly questioning,
    If I lack'd anything.

A guest, I answer'd, worthy to be here:
    Love said, You shall be he.
I the unkinde, ungrateful? Ah my deare,
    I cannot look on thee.
Love took my hand, and smiling did reply,
    Who made the eyes but I?

Truth Lord, but I have marr'd them: let my shame
    Go where it doth deserve.
And know you not, sayes Love, who bore the blame?
    My deare, then I will serve.
You must sit down, says Love, and taste my meat:
    So I did sit and eat.

Virtue

George Herbert

Sweet day, so cool, so calm, so bright,
The bridal of the earth and sky,
The dew shall weep thy fall tonight;
    For thou must die.

Sweet rose, whose hue angry and brave
Bids the rash gazer wipe his eye,
Thy root is ever in its grave,
    And thou must die.

Sweet spring, full of sweet days and roses,
A box where sweets compacted lie,
My music shows ye have your closes,
    And all must die.

Only a sweet and virtuous soul,
Like season'd timber, never gives;
But, though the whole world turn to coal,
    Then chiefly lives.

I loved her like the leaves

Kakinonoto Hitomaro

I loved her like the leaves,
The lush green leaves of spring
That pulled down the willows
on the bank's edge
where we walked
while she was of this world.
I built my life on her.
But man cannot flout
the laws of this world.
To the shimmering wide fields
hidden by the white cloud,
white as white silk scarf
she soared away like the morning bird,
hid from our world like the setting sun.
The child, the gift she left behind –
he cries for food; but always
finding nothing that I might give him,
I pick him up and hold him in my arms.
On the pillows where we lay,
My wife and I, as one,
I pass the daylight lonely till the dusk,
the black night sighing till the dawn.
I grieve and grieve and know no remedy.
I ache and know no road where I might meet her.

Resurrection
Vladimír Holan

Is it true that after this life of ours we shall one
   day be awakened
by a terrifying clamour of trumpets?
Forgive me, God, but I console myself
that the beginning and resurrection of all of us dead
will simply be announced by the crowing of a cock.

After that we'll remain lying down a while . . .
The first to get up
will be Mother . . . We'll hear her
quietly laying the fire,
quietly putting the kettle on the stove
and cosily taking the teapot out of the cupboard.
We'll be home once more.
      (Translated from the Czech by George Theiner)

No worst, there is none
Gerard Manley Hopkins

No worst, there is none. Pitched past pitch of grief,
More pangs will, schooled at forepangs, wilder wring.
Comforter, where, where is your comforting?
Mary, mother of us, where is your relief?
My cries heave, herds-long, huddle in a main, a chief-
Woe, world-sorrow; on an age-old anvil wince and sing-
Then lull, then leave off. Fury had shrieked 'No ling-
ering! Let me be fell: force I must be brief.'

  O the mind, mind has mountains; cliffs of fall
Frightful, sheer, no-man-fathomed. Hold them cheap
May who ne'er hung there. Nor does long our small
Durance deal with that steep or deep. Here! creep,
Wretch, under a comfort serves in a whirlwind: all
Life death does end and each day dies with sleep.

Into the hour
Elizabeth Jennings

I have come into the hour of a white healing.
Grief's surgery is over and I wear
The scar of my remorse and of my feeling.

I have come into a sudden sunlit hour
When ghosts are scared to corners. I have come
Into the time when grief begins to flower

Into a new love. It had filled my room
Long before I recognized it. Now
I speak its name. Grief finds its good way home.

The apple-blossom's handsome on the bough
And Paradise spreads round. I touch its grass.
I want to celebrate but don't know how.

I need not speak though everyone I pass
Stares at me kindly. I would put my hand
Into their hands. Now I have lost my loss

In some way I may later understand.
I hear the singing of the summer grass.
And love, I find, has no considered end,

Nor is it subject to the wilderness
Which follows death. I am not traitor to
A person or a memory. I trace

Behind that love another which is running
Around, ahead. I need not ask its meaning.

From *The Letters*
Samuel Johnson

They that mean to make no use of friends, will be at little trouble to gain them; and to be without friendship, is to be without one of the first comforts of our present state. To have no assistance from other minds, in resolving doubts, in appeasing scruples, in balancing deliberations, is a very wretched destitution. There is no wisdom in useless and hopeless sorrow, but there is something in it so like virtue, that he who is wholly without it cannot be loved, nor . . . be thought worthy of esteem. The loss of such a friend as has been taken from us increases our need of one another, and ought to unite us more closely.

Death does not come from outside
Jaan Kaplinski

Death does not come from outside. Death is within.
Born-grows together with us.
Goes with us to kindergarten and school.
Learns with us to read and count.
Goes sledging with us, and to the pictures.
Seeks with us the meaning of life.
Tries to make sense with us of Einstein and Wiener.
Makes with us our first sexual contacts.
Marries, bears children, quarrels, makes up.
Separates, or perhaps not, with us.
Goes to work, goes to the doctor, goes camping,
to the convalescent home and the sanatorium. Grows old,
sees children married, retired,
looks after grandchildren, grows ill, dies
with us. Let us not fear, then. Our death
will not outlive us.

(Translated from the Estonian by Hildi Hawkins)

Darling

Jackie Kay

You might forget the exact sound of her voice
or how her face looked when sleeping.
You might forget the sound of her quiet weeping
curled into the shape of a half moon,

when smaller that her self, she seemed already to be
   leaving
before she left, when the blossom was on the trees
and the sun was out, and all seemed good in the world.
I held her hand and sang a song from when I was a
   girl –

Heel y'ho boys, let her go boys –
and when I stopped singing she had slipped away,
already a slip of a girl again, skipping off,
her heart light, her face almost smiling.

And what I didn't know or couldn't say then
was that she hadn't really gone.
The dead don't go till you do, loved ones.
The dead are still here holding our hands.

I see you dancing, father
Brendan Kennelly

No sooner downstairs after the night's rest
And in the door
Than you started to dance a step
In the middle of the kitchen floor.

And as you danced
You whistled.
You made your own music
Always in tune with yourself.

Well, nearly always, anyway.
You're buried now
In Lislaughtin Abbey
And whenever I think of you

I go back beyond the old man
Mind and body broken
To find the unbroken man.
It is the moment before the dance begins,

Your lips are enjoying themselves
Whistling in the air.
Whatever happens or cannot happen
In the time I have to spare
I see you dancing, father.

The good

Brendan Kennelly

The good are vulnerable
As any bird in flight,
They do not think of safety,
Are blind to possible extinction
And when most vulnerable
Are most themselves.
The good are real as the sun,
Are best perceived through clouds
Of casual corruption
That cannot kill the luminous sufficiency
That shines on city, sea and wilderness,
Fastidiously revealing
One man to another,
Who yet will not accept
Responsibilities of light.
The good incline to praise,
To have the knack of seeing that
The best is not destroyed
Although forever threatened.
The good go naked in all weathers,
And by their nakedness rebuke
The small protective sanities
That hide men from themselves.
The good are difficult to see
Though open, rare, destructible;
Always, they retain a kind of youth,
The vulnerable grace

Of any bird in flight,
Content to be itself,
Accomplished master and potential victim,
Accepting what the earth or sky intends.
I think that I know one or two
Among my friends.

Let evening come

Jane Kenyon

Let the light of late afternoon
shine through chinks in the barn, moving
up the bales as the sun moves down.

Let the cricket take up chafing
as a woman takes up her needles
and her yarn. Let evening come.

Let dew collect on the hoe abandoned
in long grass. Let the stars appear
and the moon disclose her silver horn.

Let the fox go back to its sandy den.
Let the wind die down. Let the shed
go black inside. Let evening come.

To the bottle in the ditch, to the scoop
in the oats, to air in the lung
let evening come.

Let it come, as it will, and don't
be afraid. God does not leave us
comfortless, so let evening come.

Notes from the other side
Jane Kenyon

I divested myself of despair
and fear when I came here.

Now there is no more catching
one's own eye in the mirror,

there are no bad books, no plastic,
no insurance premiums, and of course

no illness. Contrition
does not exist, nor gnashing

of teeth. No one howls as the first
clod of earth hits the casket.

The poor we no longer have with us.
Our calm hearts strike only the hour,

and God, as promised, proves
to be mercy clothed in light.

The widower

Rudyard Kipling

For a season there must be pain –
For a little, little space
I shall lose the sight of her face,
Take back the old life again
While She is at rest in her place.
For a season this pain must endure,
For a little, little while
I shall sigh more often than smile
Till Time shall work me a cure,
And the pitiful days beguile.
For that season we must be apart,
For a little length of years,
Till my life's last hour nears,
And, above the beat of my heart,
I hear Her voice in my ears.
But I shall not understand –
Being set on some later love,
Shall not know her for whom I strove,
Till she reach me forth her hand,
Saying, 'Who but I have the right?'
And out of a troubled night
Shall draw me safe to the land.

Of *you*

Norman MacCaig

When the little devil, panic,
begins to grin and jump about
in my heart, in my brain, in my muscles,
I am shown the path I had lost
in the mountainy mist.

I'm writing of you.

When the pain that will kill me
is about to be unbearable,
a cool hand
puts a tablet on my tongue and the pain
dwindles away and vanishes.

I'm writing of you.

There are fires to be suffered,
the blaze of cruelty, the smoulder
of inextinguishable longing, even
the gentle candleflame of peace
that burns too.

I suffer them. I survive.

I'm writing of you.

Praise of a man
Norman MacCaig

He went through a company like a lamplighter –
see the dull minds, one after another,
begin to glow, to shed
a beneficent light.

He went through a company like
a knifegrinder – see the dull minds
scattering sparks of themselves,
becoming razory, becoming useful.

He went through a company
as himself. But now he's one
of the multitudinous company of the dead
where are no individuals.

The beneficent lights dim
but don't vanish. The razory edges
dull, but still cut. He's gone: but you can see
his tracks still, in the snow of the world.

Meeting point
Louis MacNeice

Time was away and somewhere else,
There were two glasses and two chairs
And two people with the one pulse
(Somebody stopped the moving stairs):
Time was away and somewhere else.

And they were neither up nor down;
The stream's music did not stop
Flowing through heather, limpid brown,
Although they sat in a coffee shop
And they were neither up nor down.

The bell was silent in the air
Holding its inverted poise –
Between the clang and clang a flower,
A brazen calyx of no noise:
The bell was silent in the air.

The camels crossed the miles of sand
That stretched around the cups and plates;
The desert was their own, they planned
To portion out the stars and dates:
The camels crossed the miles of sand.

Time was away and somewhere else.
The waiter did not come, the clock
Forgot them and the radio waltz
Came out like water from a rock:
Time was away and somewhere else.

Her fingers flicked away the ash
That bloomed again in tropic trees:
Not caring if the markets crash
When they had forests such as these,
Her fingers flicked away the ash.

God or whatever means the Good
Be praised that time can stop like this,
That what the heart has understood
Can verify in the body's peace
God or whatever means the Good.

Time was away and she was here
And life no longer what it was,
The bell was silent in the air
And all the room one glow because
Time was away and she was here.

The sunlight on the garden
Louis MacNeice

The sunlight on the garden
Hardens and grows cold,
We cannot cage the minute
Within its nets of gold,
When all is told
We cannot beg for pardon.

Our freedom as free lances
Advances towards its end;
The earth compels, upon it
Sonnets and birds descend;
And soon, my friend,
We shall have no time for dances.

The sky was good for flying
Defying the church bells
And every evil iron
Siren and what it tells:
The earth compels,
We are dying, Egypt, dying

And not expecting pardon,
Hardened in heart anew,
But glad to have sat under
Thunder and rain with you,
And grateful too
For sunlight on the garden.

Code poem for the French Resistance
Leo Marks

The life that I have is all that I have,
And the life that I have is yours.
The love that I have of the life that I have
Is yours and yours and yours.

A sleep I shall have
A rest I shall have,
Yet death will be but a pause,
For the peace of my years in the long green grass
Will be yours and yours and yours

À *quoi bon dire*

Charlotte Mew

Seventeen years ago you said
      Something that sounded like Good-bye;
      And everybody thinks you are dead,
          But I.

      So I, as I grow stiff and cold
To this and that say Good-bye too;
      And everybody sees that I am old
          But you.

      And one fine morning in a sunny lane
Some boy and girl will meet and kiss and swear
      That nobody can love their way again
         While over there
You will have smiled, I shall have tossed your hair.

From *The House at Pooh Corner*
A. A. Milne

Then, suddenly again, Christopher Robin, who was still looking at the world, with his chin in his hands, called out 'Pooh!'

'Yes?' said Pooh.

'When I'm - when—Pooh!'

'Yes, Christopher Robin?'

'I'm not going to do Nothing any more.'

'Never again?'

'Well, not so much. They don't let you.'

Pooh waited for him to go on, but he was silent again.

'Yes, Christopher Robin?' said Pooh helpfully.

'Pooh, when I'm - *you* know - when I'm *not* doing Nothing, will you come up here sometimes?'

'Just me?'

'Yes, Pooh.'

'Will you be here too?'

'Yes, Pooh, I will be *really*. I *promise* I will be, Pooh.'

'That's good,' said Pooh.

'Pooh, *promise* you won't forget about me, ever. Not even when I'm a hundred.'

Pooh thought for a little.

'How old shall *I* be then?'

'Ninety-nine.'

Pooh nodded.

'I promise,' he said.

Still with his eyes on the world Christopher Robin put out a hand and felt Pooh's paw.

'Pooh,' said Christopher Robin earnestly, 'if I – if I'm not quite–' he stopped and tried again – 'Pooh, *whatever* happens, you *will* understand, won't you?'

'Understand what?'

'Oh, nothing.' He laughed and jumped to his feet. 'Come on!'

'Where?' said Pooh.

'Anywhere.' said Christopher Robin.

So they went off together. But wherever they go, and whatever happens to them on the way, in that enchanted place on the top of the Forest, a little boy and his Bear will always be playing.

The way
Edwin Muir

Friend, I have lost the way.
The way leads on.
Is there another way?
The way is one.
I must retrace the track.
It's lost and gone.
Back, I must travel back!
None goes there, none.
Then I'll make here my place,
(The road leads on),
Stand still and set my face,
(The road leaps on),
Stay here, for ever stay.
None stays here, none.
I cannot find the way.
The way leads on.
Oh places I have passed!
That journey's done.
And what will come at last?
The road leads on.

Sonnet LXXXIX

Pablo Neruda

When I die, I want your hands on my eyes:
I want the light and the wheat of your beloved hands
to pass their freshness over me once more:
I want to feel the softness that changed my destiny.

I want you to live while I wait for you, asleep
I want your ears still to hear the wind, I want you
to sniff the sea's aroma that we loved together,
to continue to walk on the sand we walk on.

I want what I love to continue to live,
and you whom I love and sang above everything else
to continue to nourish, full-flowered:

so that you can reach everything my love directs you to,
so that my shadow can travel along in your hair,
so that everything can learn the reason for my song.

(Translated from the Spanish by Stephen Tapscott)

This is what I wanted to sign off with
Alden Nowlan

You know what I'm
like when I'm sick: I'd sooner
curse than cry. And people don't often
know what they're saying in the end.
Or I could die in my sleep.

So I'll say it now. Here it is.
Don't pay any attention
if I don't get it right
when it's for real. Blame that
on terror and pain
or the stuff they're shooting
into my veins. This is what I wanted to
sign off with. Bend
closer, listen, I love you.

Light *(for Ciaran)*
Hugh O'Donnell

My little man, down what centuries
of light did you travel
to reach us here,
your stay so short-lived;

in the twinkling of an eye
you were moving on,
bearing our name and a splinter
of the human cross we suffer;

flashed upon us like a beacon,
we wait in darkness for that light
to come round, knowing at heart
you shine forever for us.

A *quiet soul*

John Oldham

Thy soul within such silent pomp did keep,
As if humanity were lull'd asleep;
So gentle was thy pilgrimage beneath,
Time's unheard feet scarce make less noise,
Or the soft journey which a planet goes:
Life seem'd all calm as its last breath.
A still tranquillity so hush'd thy breast,
As if some Halcyon were its guest,
And there had built her nest;
It hardly now enjoys a greater rest.

In Blackwater Woods

Mary Oliver

Look, the trees
are turning
their own bodies
into pillars

of light,
are giving off the rich
fragrance of cinnamon
and fulfillment,

the long tapers
of cattails
are bursting and floating away over
the blue shoulders

of the ponds,
and every pond,
no matter what its
name is, is

nameless now.
Every year
everything
I have ever learned

in my lifetime
leads back to this: the fires
and the black river of loss
whose other side

is salvation,
whose meaning
none of us will ever know.
To live in this world

you must be able
to do three things:
to love what is mortal;
to hold it

against your bones knowing
your own life depends on it;
and, when the time comes to let it go,
to let it go.

When death comes

Mary Oliver

When death comes
like the hungry bear in autumn;
when death comes and takes all the bright coins from his purse

to buy me, and snaps the purse shut;
when death comes
like the measle-pox;

when death comes
like an iceberg between the shoulder blades,

I want to step through the door full of curiosity, wondering:
what is it going to be like, that cottage of darkness?

And therefore I look upon everything
as a brotherhood and a sisterhood,
and I look upon time as no more than an idea,
and I consider eternity as another possibility,

and I think of each life as a flower, as common
as a field daisy, and as singular,

and each name a comfortable music in the mouth,
tending, as all music does, toward silence,

and each body a lion of courage, and something
precious to the earth.

When it's over, I want to say: all my life
I was a bride married to amazement.
I was the bridegroom, taking the world into my arms.

When it's over, I don't want to wonder
if I have made of my life something particular, and real.
I don't want to find myself sighing and frightened,
or full of argument.

I don't want to end up simply having visited this world.

It is here (for A)
Harold Pinter

What sound was that?
I turn away, into the shaking room.

What was that sound that came in on the dark?
What is this maze of light it leaves us in?
What is this stance we take,
To turn away and then turn back?
What did we hear?

It was the breath
we took when we first met.
Listen. It is here.

The dying Christian to his soul
Alexander Pope

> Vital spark of heav'nly flame!
> Quit, oh quit this mortal frame:
> Trembling, hoping, ling'ring, flying,
> Oh the pain, the bliss of dying!
> Cease, fond Nature, cease thy strife,
> And let me languish into life.

> Hark! they whisper; Angels say,
> 'Sister Spirit, come away!'
> What is this absorbs me quite?
> Steals my senses, shuts my sight,
> Drowns my spirits, draws my breath?
> Tell me, my Soul, can this be Death?

> The world recedes; it disappears!
> Heav'n opens on my eyes! my ears
> With sounds seraphic ring:
> Lend, lend your wings! I mount! I fly!
> O Grave! where is thy Victory?
> O Death! where is thy Sting?

Taking leave of a friend
Ezra Pound

Blue mountains to the north of the walls,
White river winding about them;
Here we must make separation
And go out through a thousand miles of dead grass.
Mind like a floating wide cloud,
Sunset like the parting of old acquaintances
Who bow over their clasped hands at a distance.
Our horses neigh to each other
      as we are departing.

From *Remembrance of Things Past*
Marcel Proust

It is often said that something may survive of a person after his death, if that person was an artist and put a little of himself into his work. It is perhaps in the same way that a sort of cutting taken from one person and grafted on to the heart of another continues to carry on its existence even when the person from whom it had been detached has perished.

Love constant beyond death
Francisco de Quevedo

Though my eyes be closed by the final
Shadow that sweeps me off on the blank white day
And thus my soul be rendered up
By fawning time to hastening death;

Yet memory will not abandon love
On the shore where it first burned:
My flame can swim through coldest water
And will not bend to laws severe.

Soul that was prison to a god,
Veins that fuelled such fire,
Marrow that gloriously burned –

The body they will leave, though not its cares;
Ash they will be, but filled with meaning;
Dust they will be, but dust in love.

(Translated from the Spanish
by Margaret Jull Costa)

Remember

Christina G. Rossetti

Remember me when I am gone away,
      Gone far away into the silent land;
      When you can no more hold me by the hand,
Nor I half turn to go yet turning stay.
Remember me when no more day by day
      You tell me of our future that you planned:
      Only remember me; you understand
It will be late to counsel then or pray.
Yet if you should forget me for a while
      And afterwards remember, do not grieve:
      For if the darkness and corruption leave
      A vestige of the thoughts that once I had,
Better by far you should forget and smile
      Than that you should remember and be sad.

Everything you see
Rumi

Everything you see has its roots in the unseen world.
　　　The forms may change, yet the essence remains
　　　　the same.
Every wonderful sight will vanish, every sweet word
　　will fade,
　　　But do not be disheartened,
The source they come from is eternal, growing,
　　　Branching out, giving new life and new joy.
Why do you weep?
　　　The source is within you
And this whole world is springing up from it.

From *Cymbeline* – Act 4, Scene 2
William Shakespeare

Fear no more the heat o' th' sun,
  Nor the furious winter's rages,
Thou thy worldly task hast done,
  Home art gone and ta'en thy wages.
Golden lads and girls all must,
As chimney-sweepers, come to dust.

Fear no more the frown o' th' great,
  Thou art past the tyrant's stroke
Care no more to clothe and eat,
  To thee the reed is as the oak.
The sceptre, learning, physic, must
All follow this, and come to dust.

Fear no more the lightning-flash,
  Nor th' all-dreaded thunder-stone;
Fear not slander, censure rash.
  Thou hast finish'd joy and moan.
All lovers young, all lovers must
Consign to thee and come to dust.

No exorciser harm thee!
Nor no witchcraft charm thee!
Ghost unlaid forbear thee!
Nothing ill come near thee!
Quiet consummation have,
And renowned be thy grave!

From *The Tempest* – Act 4, Scene 1
William Shakespeare

Our revels now are ended. These our actors,
As I foretold you, were all spirits, and
Are melted into air, into thin air:
And, like the baseless fabric of this vision,
The cloud-capp'd towers, the gorgeous palaces,
The solemn temples, the great globe itself,
Yea, all which it inherit, shall dissolve
And, like this insubstantial pageant faded,
Leave not a rack behind. We are such stuff
As dreams are made on, and our little life
Is rounded with a sleep.

Sonnet XXIX

William Shakespeare

When, in disgrace with fortune and men's eyes,
I all alone beweep my outcast state,
And trouble deaf heaven with my bootless cries,
And look upon myself, and curse my fate,
Wishing me like to one more rich in hope,
Featured like him, like him with friends possessed,
Desiring this man's art and that man's scope,
With what I most enjoy contented least;
Yet in these thoughts myself almost despising,
Haply I think on thee - and then my state,
Like to the lark at break of day arising
From sullen earth, sings hymns at heaven's gate;
  For thy sweet love rememb'red such wealth brings
  That then I scorn to change my state with kings.

Sonnet XXX

William Shakespeare

When to the sessions of sweet silent thought
I summon up remembrance of things past,
I sigh the lack of many a thing I sought,
And with old woes new wail my dear times' waste;
Then can I drown an eye, unus'd to flow,
For precious friends hid in death's dateless night,
And weep afresh love's long since cancell'd woe,
And moan the expense of many a vanish'd sight:
Then can I grieve at grievances foregone,
And heavily from woe to woe tell o'er
The sad account of fore-bemoanéd moan,
Which I new pay as if not paid before.
   But if the while I think on thee, dear friend,
   All losses are restor'd and sorrows end.

From *Adonais*

Percy Bysshe Shelley

Peace, peace! he is not dead, he doth not sleep –
He hath awakened from the dream of life –
'Tis we, who lost in stormy visions, keep
With phantoms an unprofitable strife,
And in mad trance, strike with our spirit's knife
Invulnerable nothings – *We* decay
Like corpses in a charnel; fear and grief
Convulse us and consume us day by day,
And cold hopes swarm like worms within our living clay.

He has outsoared the shadow of our night;
Envy and calumny and hate and pain,
And that unrest which men miscall delight,
Can touch him not and torture not again;
From the contagion of the world's slow stain
He is secure, and now can never mourn
A heart grown cold, a head grown gray in vain;
Nor, when the spirit's self has ceased to burn,
With sparkless ashes load an unlamented urn.

Music

Percy Bysshe Shelley

Music, when soft voices die,
Vibrates in the memory –
Odours, when sweet violets sicken,
Live within the sense they quicken.
Rose leaves, when the rose is dead,
Are heaped for the beloved's bed;
And so thy thoughts, when thou art gone,
Love itself shall slumber on.

The truly great
Stephen Spender

I think continually of those who were truly great.
Who, from the womb, remembered the soul's history
Through corridors of light, where the hours are suns,
Endless and singing. Whose lovely ambition
Was that their lips, still touched with fire,
Should tell of the Spirit, clothed from head to foot in
　　　song.
And who hoarded from the Spring branches
The desires falling across their bodies like blossoms.

What is precious, is never to forget
The essential delight of the blood drawn from ageless
　　　springs
Breaking through rocks in worlds before our earth.
Never to deny its pleasure in the morning simple light
Nor its grave evening demand for love.
Never to allow gradually the traffic to smother
With noise and fog, the flowering of the Spirit.

Near the snow, near the sun, in the highest fields,
See how these names are fêted by the waving grass
And by the streamers of white cloud
And whispers of wind in the listening sky.
The names of those who in their lives fought for life,
Who wore at their hearts the fire's centre.
Born of the sun, they travelled a short while toward
　　　the sun
And left the vivid air signed with their honour.

Peace, my heart
Rabindranath Tagore

Peace, my heart, let the time for the parting be sweet.
Let it not be a death but completeness.
Let love melt into memory and pain into songs.
Let the flight through the sky end in the folding of
the wings over the nest.
Let the last touch of your hands be gentle like the
flower of the night.
Stand still, O Beautiful End, for a moment, and say
your last words in silence.
I bow to you and hold up my lamp to light you on
your way.

Farewell my friends

Rabindranath Tagore

It was beautiful
As long as it lasted
The journey of my life.
I have no regrets
Whatsoever said
The pain I'll leave behind.
Those dear hearts
Who love and care . . .
And the strings pulling
At the heart and soul . . .
The strong arms
That held me up
When my own strength
Let me down.
At the turning of my life
I came across
Good friends,
Friends who stood by me
Even when time raced me by.
Farewell, farewell my friends
I smile and
Bid you goodbye.
No, shed no tears
For I need them not
All I need is your smile.
If you feel sad
Do think of me

For that's what I'll like
When you live in the hearts
Of those you love
Remember then
You never die.

Those who are near me do not know
Rabindranath Tagore

They who are near me do not know that you are
  nearer to me than they are
Those who speak to me do not know that my heart is
  full with your unspoken words
Those who crowd in my path do not know that I am
  walking alone with you
They who love me do not know that their love brings
  you to my heart.

Crossing the bar
Alfred, Lord Tennyson

Sunset and evening star,
    And one clear call for me!
And may there be no moaning of the bar,
    When I put out to sea,

But such a tide as moving seems asleep,
    Too full for sound and foam,
When that which drew from out the boundless deep
    Turns again home.

Twilight and evening bell,
    And after that the dark!
And may there be no sadness of farewell,
    When I embark;

For though from out our bourne of Time and Place
    The flood may bear me far,
I hope to see my Pilot face to face
    When I have crost the bar.

From *In Memoriam* A. H. H. - VII
Alfred, Lord Tennyson

Dark house, by which once more I stand
    Here in the long unlovely street,
    Doors, where my heart was used to beat
So quickly, waiting for a hand,

A hand that can be clasped no more -
    Behold me, for I cannot sleep,
    And like a guilty thing I creep
At earliest morning to the door.

He is not here; but far away
    The noise of life begins again,
    And ghastly through the drizzling rain
On the bald street breaks the blank day.

From *In Memoriam* A. H. H. - XXVII
Alfred, Lord Tennyson

I envy not in any moods
     The captive void of noble rage,
     The linnet born within the cage,
That never knew the summer woods:

I envy not the beast that takes
     His license in the field of time,
     Unfettered by the sense of crime,
To whom a conscience never wakes;

Nor, what may count itself as blest,
     The heart that never plighted troth
     But stagnates in the weeds of sloth;
Nor any want-begotten rest.

I hold it true, whate'er befall;
     I feel it, when I sorrow most;
     'Tis better to have loved and lost
Than never to have loved at all.

And death shall have no dominion
Dylan Thomas

And death shall have no dominion.
Dead men naked they shall be one
With the man in the wind and the west moon;
When their bones are picked clean and the
    clean bones gone,
They shall have stars at elbow and foot;
Though they go mad they shall be sane,
Though they sink through the sea they shall
    rise again;
Though lovers be lost love shall not;
And death shall have no dominion.

And death shall have no dominion.
Under the windings of the sea
They lying long shall not die windily;
Twisting on racks when sinews give way,
Strapped to a wheel, yet they shall not break;
Faith in their hands shall snap in two,
And the unicorn evils run them through;
Split all ends up they shan't crack;
And death shall have no dominion.

And death shall have no dominion.
No more may gulls cry at their ears
Or waves break loud on the seashores;
Where blew a flower may a flower no more
Lift its head to the blows of the rain;

Though they be mad and dead as nails,
Heads of the characters hammer through daisies;
Break in the sun till the sun breaks down,
And death shall have no dominion.

Do not go gentle into that good night
Dylan Thomas

Do not go gentle into that good night,
Old age should burn and rave at close of day;
Rage, rage against the dying of the light.

Though wise men at their end know dark is right,
Because their words had forked no lightning they
Do not go gentle into that good night.

Good men, the last wave by, crying how bright
Their frail deeds might have danced in a green bay,
Rage, rage against the dying of the light.

Wild men who caught and sang the sun in flight,
And learn, too late, they grieved it on its way,
Do not go gentle into that good night.

Grave men, near death, who see with blinding sight
Blind eyes could blaze like meteors and be gay,
Rage, rage against the dying of the light.

And you, my father, there on the sad height,
Curse, bless, me now with your fierce tears, I pray.
Do not go gentle into that good night.
Rage, rage against the dying of the light.

Comparisons

R. S. Thomas

To all light things
I compared her; to
a snowflake, a feather.

I remember she rested
at the dance on my
arm, as a bird

on its nest lest
the eggs break, lest
she lean too heavily

on our love. Snow
melts, feathers
are blown away;

I have let
her ashes down
in me like an anchor.

Belief

Ann Thorp

I have to believe
That you still exist
Somewhere,
That you still watch me
Sometimes,
That you still love me
Somehow.

I have to believe
That life has meaning
Somehow,
That I am useful here
Sometimes,
That I make small differences
Somewhere.

I have to believe
That I need to stay here
For some time,
That all this teaches me
Something,
So that I can meet you again
Somewhere.

The parting glass
Traditional Irish

Of all the money that e'er I spent,
I spent it in good company;
And any harm that e'er I've done,
I trust it was to none but me;
May those I've loved through all the years
Have memories now they'll e'er recall;
So fill to me the parting glass,
Goodnight, and joy be with you all.

Oh all the comrades that e'er I had,
Are sorry for my going away;
And all the loved ones that e'er I had
Would wish me one more day to stay.
But since it falls unto my lot
That I should leave and you should not,
I'll gently rise and I'll softly call
Goodnight, and joy be with you all.

Of all good times that e'er we shared,
I leave to you fond memory;
And for all the friendship that e'er we had
I ask you to remember me;
And when you sit and stories tell,
I'll be with you and help recall;
So fill to me the parting glass,
God bless, and joy be with you all.

From *Thanksgivings for the body*
Thomas Traherne

O what praises are due unto Thee,
    Who has made me
        A living inhabitant
           Of the great world.
      And the centre of it!
    A sphere of sense,
        And a mine of riches,
Which when bodies are dissected fly away.
    The spacious room
        Which Thou has hidden in mine eye,
    The chambers for sounds
        Which Thou has prepar'd in mine ear,
    The receptacles for smells
        Concealed in my nose;
    The feeling of my hands,
        The taste of my tongue.
    But above all, O Lord, the glory of speech,
whereby Thy servant is enabled with praise to
celebrate Thee.
                For
    All the beauties in Heaven and earth,
    The melody of sounds,
    The sweet odours
        Of Thy dwelling-place.
    The delectable pleasures that gratify my sense,
        That gratify the feeling of mankind.
    The light of history,
        Admitted by the ear.

The light of Heaven,
                    Brought in by the eye.
The volubility and liberty
                    Of my hands and members.
Fitted by Thee for all operations;
                    Which the fancy can imagine,
                    Or soul desire:
From the framing of a needle's eye,
                    To the building of a tower:
From the squaring of trees,
                    To the polishing of kings' crowns.
For all the mysteries, engines, instruments,
wherewith the world is filled, which we are able
to frame and use to Thy glory.
For all the trades, variety of operations, cities,
temples, streets, bridges, mariner's compass,
admirable pictures, sculpture, writing, printing,
songs and music, wherewith the world is
beautified and adorned.

Time is

Henry Van Dyke

Time is too slow for those who wait,
too swift for those who fear,
too long for those who grieve,
too short for those who rejoice;
but for those who love, time is eternity.

They are all gone into the world of light!
Henry Vaughan

They are all gone into the world of light!
    And I alone sit lingering here;
Their very memory is fair and bright,
        And my sad thoughts doth clear.

It glows and glitters in my cloudy breast
    Like stars upon some gloomy grove,
Or those faint beams in which this hill is drest,
        After the Sun's remove.

I see them walking in an Air of glory,
    Whose light doth trample on my days:
My days, which are at best but dull and hoary,
        Mere glimmering and decays.

O holy hope! and high humility,
    High as the Heavens above!
These are your walks, and you have shew'd them me
        To kindle my cold love,

Dear, beauteous death! the Jewel of the Just,
    Shining nowhere, but in the dark;
What mysteries do lie beyond thy dust;
        Could man outlook that mark!

He that hath found some fledg'd birds nest, may know
    At first sight, if the bird be flown;
But what fair Well or Grove he sings in now,
        That is to him unknown.

And yet, as Angels in some brighter dreams
      Call to the soul, when man doth sleep:
So some strange thoughts transcend our wonted themes,
      And into glory peep.

If a star were confin'd into a Tomb,
      Her captive flames must needs burn there;
But when the hand that lock'd her up, gives room,
      She'll shine through all the sphere.

O Father of eternal life, and all
      Created glories under thee!
Resume thy spirit from this world of thrall
      Into true liberty.

Either disperse these mists, which blot and fill
      My perspective (still) as they pass,
Or else remove me hence unto that hill,
      Where I shall need no glass.

Good night, Willie Lee,
I'll see you in the morning
Alice Walker

Looking down into my father's
dead face
for the last time
my mother said without
tears, without smiles
without regrets
but with civility
'Good night, Willie Lee, I'll see you
in the morning.'
And it was then I knew that the healing
of all our wounds
is forgiveness
that permits a promise
of our return
at the end.

Of the last verses in the book
Edmund Waller

When we for Age could neither read nor write,
The Subject made us able to indite.
The Soul, with Nobler Resolutions deckt,
The Body stooping, does Herself erect:
No Mortal Parts are requisite to raise
Her, that Unbody'd can her Maker praise.

The Seas are quiet, when the Winds give o'er;
So calm are we, when Passions are no more:
For then we know how vain it was to boast
Of fleeting Things, so certain to be lost.
Clouds of Affection from our younger Eyes
Conceal that emptiness, which Age descries.

The Soul's dark Cottage, batter'd and decay'd,
Lets in new Light thrò chinks that time has made;
Stronger by weakness, wiser Men become
As they draw near to their Eternal home:
Leaving the Old, both Worlds at once they view,
That stand upon the Threshold of the New.

From *When lilacs last in the dooryard bloom'd*

Walt Whitman

10

O how shall I warble myself for the dead one there
    I loved?
And how shall I deck my song for the large sweet
    soul that has gone?
And what shall my perfume be for the grave of
    him I love?

Sea-winds blown from east and west,
Blown from the Eastern sea and blown from the
Western sea, till there on the prairies meeting,
These and with these and the breath of my chant,
I'll perfume the grave of him I love.

The baton
Anna Wigley

How smoothly you handed on the baton.
As if you'd known the time and place
and kept it secret from us; then
when the moment came, yielded it up
saying *Take it, quick, I cannot hold it,*
and let it swiftly slip your grasp.
We were left looking down at your empty hands,
the worn, surrendered fingers,
and a weight that had suddenly shifted.

From *The Prelude*

William Wordsworth

Whether we be young or old,
Our destiny, our being's heart and home,
Is with infinitude, and only there;
With hope it is, hope that can never die,
Effort, and expectation, and desire,
And something evermore about to be.

Farewell, sweet dust
Elinor Wylie

Now I have lost you, I must scatter
All of you on the air henceforth;
Not that to me it can ever matter
But it's only fair to the rest of the earth.

Now especially, when it is winter
And the sun's not half as bright as it was,
Who wouldn't be glad to find a splinter
That once was you, in the frozen grass?

Snowflakes, too, will be softer feathered,
Clouds, perhaps, will be whiter plumed;
Rain, whose brilliance you caught and gathered,
Purer silver have resumed.

Farewell, sweet dust; I never was a miser:
Once, for a minute, I made you mine:
Now you are gone, I am none the wiser
But the leaves of the willow are as bright as wine.

Only a little while

Yakamochi

We were together
Only a little while,
And we believed our love
Would last a thousand years.

Hymns

Abide with me

H. F. Lyte

Abide with me; fast falls the eventide;
The darkness deepens; Lord, with me abide!
When other helpers fail, and comforts flee,
Help of the helpless, O abide with me.

Swift to its close ebbs out life's little day;
Earth's joys grow dim, its glories pass away;
Change and decay in all around I see;
O thou who changest not, abide with me.

I need thy presence every passing hour;
What but thy grace can foil the tempter's power?
Who like thyself my guide and stay can be?
Through cloud and sunshine, O abide with me.

I fear no foe with thee at hand to bless;
Ills have no weight, and tears no bitterness.
Where is death's sting? where, grave, thy victory?
I triumph still, if thou abide with me.

Hold thou thy cross before my closing eyes;
Shine through the gloom, and point me to the skies:
Heaven's morning breaks, and earth's vain shadows flee;
In life, in death, O Lord, abide with me!

All creatures of our God and King

St Francis of Assisi, trans. William Draper

All creatures of our God and King,
Lift up your voice and with us sing
Alleluya, alleluya!
Thou burning sun with golden beam,
Thou silver moon with softer gleam:

Refrain
O praise him, O praise him,
Alleluya, Alleluya, Alleluya!

Thou rushing wind that art so strong,
Ye clouds that sail in heaven along,
O praise him, Alleluya!
Thou rising morn, in praise rejoice,
Ye lights of evening, find a voice: Refrain

Thou flowing water, pure and clear,
Make music for thy Lord to hear,
Alleluya, Alleluya!
Thou fire so masterful and bright,
That givest man both warmth and light: Refrain

Dear mother earth, who day by day
Unfoldest blessings on our way,
O praise him, Alleluya!
The flowers and fruits that in thee grow,
Let them his glory also show: Refrain

And all ye men of tender heart,
Forgiving others, take your part,
O sing ye, Alleluya!
Ye who long pain and sorrow bear,
Praise God and on him cast your care: Refrain

And thou, most kind and gentle death,
Waiting to hush our latest breath,
O praise him, Alleluya!
Thou leadest home the child of God,
And Christ our Lord the way hath trod: Refrain

Let all things their Creator bless,
And worship him in humbleness,
O praise him, Alleluya!
Praise, praise the Father, praise the Son,
And praise the Spirit, three in One:

   O praise him, O praise him,
   Alleluya, Alleluya, Alleluya!

All things bright and beautiful
C. F. Alexander

Refrain:
All things bright and beautiful,
All creatures great and small,
All things wise and wonderful,
The Lord God made them all.

Each little flower that opens,
Each little bird that sings,
He made their glowing colours,
He made their tiny wings.   Refrain

The purple-headed mountain,
The river running by,
The sunset and the morning,
That brightens up the sky;   Refrain

The cold wind in the winter,
The pleasant summer sun,
The ripe fruits in the garden,
He made them every one;   Refrain

He gave us eyes to see them,
And lips that we might tell
How great is God Almighty,
Who has made all things well.   Refrain

All my hope on God is founded
Robert Bridges

All my hope on God is founded;
He doth still my trust renew.
Me through change and chance he guideth,
Only good and only true.
God unknown,
He alone
Calls my heart to be his own.

Human pride and earthly glory,
Sword and crown betray his trust;
What with care and toil he buildeth,
Tower and temple, fall to dust
But God's power,
Hour by hour,
Is my temple and my tower.

God's great goodness aye endureth,
Deep his wisdom, passing thought:
Splendour, light and life attend him,
Beauty springeth out of naught.
Evermore
From his store
New-born worlds rise and adore.

Daily doth th' Almighty giver
Bounteous gifts on us bestow;
His desire our soul delighteth,
Pleasure leads us where we go.
Love doth stand

At his hand;
Joy doth wait on his command.

Still from earth to God eternal
Sacrifice of praise be done,
High above all praises praising
For the gift of Christ his Son.
Christ doth call
One and all:
Ye who follow shall not fall.

All ye who seek a comfort sure

Latin, eighteenth century, trans. Edward Caswall

All ye who seek a comfort sure
In trouble and distress,
Whatever sorrow vex the mind,
Or guilt the soul oppress,

Jesus, who gave himself for you
Upon the cross to die,
Opens to you his sacred heart;
O to that heart draw nigh.

Ye hear how kindly he invites;
Ye hear his words so blest –
'All ye that labour come to me,
And I will give you rest.'

O Jesus, joy of saints on high,
Thou hope of sinners here,
Attracted by those loving words
To thee I lift my prayer.

Wash thou my wounds in that dear blood
Which forth from thee doth flow;
New grace, new hope inspire, a new
And better heart bestow.

Be still my soul, the Lord is on thy side

Katherina A. D. von Schlegel,
trans. Jane Borthwick

Be still, my soul: the Lord is on thy side.
Bear patiently the cross of grief or pain.
Leave to thy God to order and provide;
In every change, He faithful will remain.
Be still, my soul: thy best, thy heav'nly Friend
Through thorny ways leads to a joyful end.

Be still, my soul: thy God doth undertake
To guide the future, as He has the past.
Thy hope, thy confidence let nothing shake;
All now mysterious shall be bright at last.
Be still, my soul: the waves and winds still know
His voice Who ruled them while He dwelt below.

Be still, my soul: when dearest friends depart,
And all is darkened in the vale of tears,
Then shalt thou better know His love, His heart,
Who comes to soothe thy sorrow and thy fears.
Be still, my soul: thy Jesus can repay
From His own fullness all He takes away.

Be still, my soul: the hour is hast'ning on
When we shall be for ever with the Lord.
When disappointment, grief, and fear are gone,
Sorrow forgot, love's purest joys restored.
Be still, my soul: when change and tears are past
All safe and blessed we shall meet at last.

Be still, my soul: begin the song of praise
On earth, believing, to Thy Lord on high;
Acknowledge Him in all thy words and ways,
So shall He view thee with a well-pleased eye.
Be still, my soul: the Sun of life divine
Through passing clouds shall but more brightly shine.

Be thou my vision, O Lord of my heart
Irish, eighth century, trans. Mary Byrne

Be thou my vision, O Lord of my heart,
Be all else but naught to me, save that thou art,
Be thou my best thought in the day and the night,
Both waking and sleeping, thy presence my light.

Be thou my wisdom, be thou my true word,
Be thou ever with me, and I with thee, Lord,
Be thou my great Father, and I thy true son,
Be thou in me dwelling, and I with thee one.

Be thou my breastplate, my sword for the fight,
Be thou my whole armour, be thou my true might,
Be thou my soul's shelter, be thou my strong tower,
O raise thou me heavenward, great Power of my power.

Riches I heed not, nor all the world's praise,
Be thou my inheritance now and always,
Be thou and thou only the first in my heart,
O Sovereign of heaven, my treasure thou art.

High King of heaven, thou heaven's bright Sun,
O grant me its joys after vict'ry is won,
Great Heart of my own heart, whatever befall,
Still be thou my vision, O Ruler of all.

Dear Lord and Father of mankind
John Whittier

Dear Lord and Father of mankind,
Forgive our foolish ways!
Re-clothe us in our rightful mind,
In purer lives thy service find,
In deeper reverence praise.

In simple trust like theirs who heard,
Beside the Syrian sea,
The gracious calling of the Lord,
Let us, like them, without a word
Rise up and follow thee.

O Sabbath rest by Galilee!
O calm of hills above,
Where Jesus knelt to share with thee
The silence of eternity,
Interpreted by love!

Drop thy still dews of quietness,
Till all our strivings cease;
Take from our souls the strain and stress,
And let our ordered lives confess
The beauty of thy peace.

Breathe through the heats of our desire
Thy coolness and thy balm;
Let sense be dumb, let flesh retire;
Speak through the earthquake, wind, and fire,
O still small voice of calm!

For all the Saints who from
their labours rest
W. Walsham How

For all the Saints who from their labours rest,
Who thee by faith before the world confest,
Thy name, O Jesu, be for ever blest.
Alleluya! Alleluya!

Thou wast their Rock, their Fortress, and their Might;
Thou, Lord, their Captain in the well fought fight;
Thou in the darkness drear their one true Light.
Alleluya! Alleluya!

O may thy soldiers, faithful, true and bold,
Fight as the Saints who nobly fought of old,
And win, with them, the victor's crown of gold.
Alleluya! Alleluya!

O blest communion! fellowship divine!
We feebly struggle, they in glory shine;
Yet all are one in thee, for all are thine.
Alleluya! Alleluya!

And when the strife is fierce, the warfare long,
Steals on the ear the distant triumph song,
And hearts are brave again, and arms are strong.
Alleluya! Alleluya!

The golden evening brightens in the west;
Soon, soon to faithful warriors cometh rest:
Sweet is the calm of Paradise the blest.
Alleluya! Alleluya!

But lo! there breaks a yet more glorious day;
The Saints triumphant rise in bright array:
The King of glory passes on his way.
Alleluya! Alleluya!

From earth's wide bounds, from ocean's farthest coast,
Through gates of pearl streams in the countless host,
Singing to Father, Son, and Holy Ghost.
Alleluya! Alleluya!

For the beauty of the earth
F. S. Pierpoint

For the beauty of the earth,
For the beauty of the skies,
For the love which from our birth
Over and around us lies:

Refrain:
Lord of all, to thee we raise
This our sacrifice of praise.

For the beauty of each hour,
Of the day and of the night,
Hill and vale, and tree and flower,
Sun and moon and stars of light: Refrain

For the joy of ear and eye,
For the heart and brain's delight,
For the mystic harmony
Linking sense to sound and sight: Refrain

For the joy of human love,
Brother, sister, parent, child,
Friends on earth and friends above,
For all gentle thoughts and mild: Refrain

For each perfect gift of thine,
To our race so freely given,
Graces human and divine,
Flowers of earth and buds of heaven: Refrain

For thy Church that evermore
Lifteth holy hands above,
Offering up on every shore
This pure sacrifice of love: Refrain

Lord of all, to thee we raise
This our sacrifice of praise.

Guide me, O thou great Redeemer
W. Williams

Guide me, O thou great Redeemer,
Pilgrim through this barren land;
I am weak, but thou art mighty,
Hold me with thy powerful hand:
Bread of heaven,   (x2)
Feed me till I want no more.   (x2)

Open now the crystal fountain
Whence the healing stream doth flow;
Let the fire and cloudy pillar
Lead me all my journey through:
Strong deliverer,   (x2)
Be thou still my strength and shield. (x2)

When I tread the verge of Jordan,
Bid my anxious fears subside;
Death of death, and hell's Destruction
Land me safe on Canaan's side:
Songs of praises   (x2)
I will ever give to thee.   (x2)

Hark, my soul, it is the Lord
William Cowper

Hark, my soul, it is the Lord;
'tis thy Saviour, hear his word;
Jesus speaks, and speaks to thee,
'Say, poor sinner, lov'st thou me?

'I delivered thee when bound,
and, when wounded, healed thy wound;
sought thee wandering, set thee right,
turned thy darkness into light.

'Can a woman's tender care
cease towards the child she bare?
Yes, she may forgetful be,
yet will I remember thee.

'Mine is an unchanging love,
higher than the heights above,
deeper than the depths beneath,
free and faithful, strong as death.

'Thou shalt see my glory soon,
when the work of grace is done;
partner of my throne shalt be:
say, poor sinner, lov'st thou me?'

Lord, it is my chief complaint,
that my love is weak and faint;
yet I love thee, and adore;
O for grace to love thee more!

He who would valiant be
John Bunyan

He who would valiant be
'Gainst all disaster,
Let him in constancy
Follow the Master.
There's no discouragement
Shall make him once relent
His first avowed intent
To be a pilgrim.

Who so beset him round
With dismal stories,
Do but themselves confound –
His strength the more is.
No foes shall stay his might,
Though he with giants fight:
He will make good the right
To be a pilgrim.

Since, Lord, thou dost defend
Us with thy Spirit,
We know we at the end
Shall life inherit.
Then fancies flee away!
I'll fear not what men say,
I'll labour night and day
To be a pilgrim.

Immortal, invisible, God only wise
W. Chalmers Smith

Immortal, invisible, God only wise,
In light inaccessible hid from our eyes,
Most blessèd, most glorious, the Ancient of Days,
Almighty, victorious, thy great name we praise.

Unresting, unhasting, and silent as light,
Nor wanting, nor wasting, thou rulest in might;
Thy justice like mountains high soaring above
Thy clouds which are fountains of goodness and love.

To all life thou givest – to both great and small;
In all life thou livest, the true life of all;
We blossom and flourish as leaves on the tree,
And wither and perish – but nought changeth thee.

Great Father of glory, pure Father of light,
Thine angels adore thee, all veiling their sight;
All laud we would render: O help us to see
'Tis only the splendour of light hideth thee.

Immortal love for ever full

John Whittier

Immortal love for ever full,
For ever flowing free,
For ever shared, for ever whole,
A never-ebbing sea!

Our outward lips confess the name,
All other names above;
Love only knoweth whence it came
And comprehendeth love.

We may not climb the heavenly steeps
To bring the Lord Christ down;
In vain we search the lowest deeps,
For him no depths can drown;

But warm, sweet, tender, even yet
A present help is he;
And faith has still its Olivet,
And love its Galilee.

The healing of his seamless dress
Is by our beds of pain;
We touch him in life's throng and press,
And we are whole again.

Through him the first fond prayers are said
Our lips of childhood frame;
The last low whispers of our dead
Are burdened with his name.

Alone, O Love ineffable,
Thy saving name is given;
To turn aside from thee is hell,
To walk with thee is heaven.

Jerusalem the golden

Bernard of Cluny, trans J. M. Neale

Jerusalem the golden,
With milk and honey blest,
Beneath thy contemplation
Sink heart and voice opprest.
I know not, O I know not,
What social joys are there,
What radiancy of glory,
What light beyond compare.

They stand, those halls of Sion,
Conjubilant with song,
And bright with many an angel,
And all the martyr throng;
The Prince is ever in them,
The daylight is serene,
The pastures of the blessèd
Are decked in glorious sheen.

There is the throne of David,
And there, from care released,
The song of them that triumph,
The shout of them that feast;
And they who, with their Leader,
Have conquered in the fight,
For ever and for ever
Are clad in robes of white.

O sweet and blessèd country,
Shall I ever see thy face?
O sweet and blessèd country,
Shall I ever win thy grace?
Exult, O dust and ashes!
The Lord shall be thy part:
His only, his for ever,
Thou shalt be, and thou art!

Jesu, Lover of my soul
Charles Wesley

Jesu, Lover of my soul,
Let me to thy bosom fly,
While the nearer waters roll,
While the tempest still is high:
Hide me, O my Saviour, hide
Till the storm of life is past;
Safe into the haven guide,
O receive my soul at last.

Other refuge have I none,
Hangs my helpless soul on thee;
Leave, ah, leave me not alone,
Still support and comfort me.
All my trust on thee is stayed,
All my help from thee I bring;
Cover my defenceless head
With the shadow of thy wing.

Thou, O Christ, art all I want,
More than all in thee I find:
Raise the fallen, cheer the faint,
Heal the sick, and lead the blind.
Just and holy is thy name,
I am all unrighteousness;
False and full of sin I am,
Thou art full of truth and grace.

Plenteous grace with thee is found,
Grace to cover all my sin;
Let the healing streams abound,
Make and keep me pure within.
Thou of life the fountain art,
Freely let me take of thee,
Spring thou up within my heart,
Rise to all eternity.

Jesus lives! thy terrors now
Christian Gellert

Jesus lives! thy terrors now
Can, O Death, no more appal us;
Jesus lives! by this we know,
Thou, O grave, canst not enthral us. Alleluya!

Jesus lives! henceforth is death
But the gate of life immortal;
This shall calm our trembling breath,
When we pass its gloomy portal. Alleluya!

Jesus lives! for us he died;
Then, alone to Jesus living,
Pure in heart may we abide,
Glory to our Saviour giving. Alleluya!

Jesus lives! our hearts know well
Nought from us his love shall sever;
Life, nor death, nor powers of hell,
Tear us from his keeping ever. Alleluya!

Jesus lives! to him the throne
Over all the world is given;
May we go where he is gone,
Rest and reign with him in heaven. Alleluya!

Lead, kindly Light, amid the encircling gloom
John Henry Newman

Lead, kindly Light, amid the encircling gloom,
Lead thou me on;
The night is dark, and I am far from home,
Lead thou me on.
Keep thou my feet; I do not ask to see
The distant scene; one step enough for me.

I was not ever thus, nor prayed that thou
Shouldst lead me on;
I loved to choose and see my path; but now
Lead thou me on.
I loved the garish day, and, spite of fears,
Pride ruled my will: remember not past years.

So long thy power hath blest me, sure it still
Will lead me on
O'er moor and fen, o'er crag and torrent, till
The night is gone,
And with the morn those angel faces smile,
Which I have loved long since, and lost awhile.

Lead us, heavenly Father, lead us
James Edmeston

Lead us, heavenly Father, lead us
O'er the world's tempestuous sea;
Guard us, guide us, keep us, feed us,
For we have no help but thee;
Yet possessing every blessing
If our God our Father be.

Saviour, breathe forgiveness o'er us,
All our weakness thou dost know;
Thou didst tread this earth before us,
Thou didst feel its keenest woe;
Self denying, death defying,
Thou to Calvary didst go.

Spirit of our God, descending,
Fill our hearts with heavenly joy;
Love with every passion blending,
Pleasure that can never cloy;
Thus provided, pardoned, guided,
Nothing can our peace destroy.

Light's abode, celestial Salem
Latin, fifteenth century, trans. J. M. Neale

Light's abode, celestial Salem,
Vision dear whence peace doth spring,
Brighter than the heart can fancy,
Mansion of the highest King;
O, how glorious are the praises
Which of thee the prophets sing!

There for ever and for ever
Alleluya is outpoured;
For unending, for unbroken
Is the feast-day of the Lord;
All is pure and all is holy
That within thy walls is stored.

There no cloud nor passing vapour
Dims the brightness of the air;
Endless noon-day, glorious noon-day,
From the Sun of suns is there;
There no night brings rest from labour,
There unknown are toil and care.

O how glorious and resplendent,
Fragile body, shalt thou be,
When endued with so much beauty,
Full of health, and strong, and free,
Full of vigour, full of pleasure
That shall last eternally!

Now with gladness, now with courage,
Bear the burden on thee laid,
That hereafter these thy labours
May with endless gifts be paid,
And in everlasting glory
Thou with joy may'st be arrayed.

Laud and honour to the Father,
Laud and honour to the Son,
Laud and honour to the Spirit,
Ever Three and ever One,
One in love, and One in splendour,
While unending ages run.

Lord of all hopefulness
Jan Struther

Lord of all hopefulness, Lord of all joy,
Whose trust ever child-like, no cares could destroy,
Be there at our waking, and give us, we pray,
Your bliss in our hearts, Lord, at the break of the day.

Lord of all eagerness, Lord of all faith,
Whose strong hands were skilled at the plane and the
    lathe,
Be there at our labours, and give us, we pray,
Your strength in our hearts, Lord, at the noon of the day.

Lord of all kindliness, Lord of all grace,
Your hands swift to welcome, your arms to embrace,
Be there at our homing, and give us, we pray,
Your love in our hearts, Lord, at the eve of the day.

Lord of all gentleness, Lord of all calm,
Whose voice is contentment, whose presence is balm,
Be there at our sleeping, and give us, we pray,
Your peace in our hearts, Lord, at the end of the day.

Love Divine, all loves excelling
Charles Wesley

Love Divine, all loves excelling,
Joy of heaven, to earth come down,   ·
Fix in us thy humble dwelling,
All thy faithful mercies crown.
Jesu, thou art all compassion,
Pure unbounded love thou art;
Visit us with thy salvation,
Enter every trembling heart.

Come, almighty to deliver,
Let us all thy life receive;
Suddenly return, and never,
Never more thy temples leave.
Thee we would be always blessing,
Serve thee as thy hosts above,
Pray, and praise thee, without ceasing,
Glory in thy perfect love.

Finish then thy new creation,
Pure and spotless let us be;
Let us see thy great salvation,
Perfectly restored in thee,
Changed from glory into glory,
Till in heaven we take our place,
Till we cast our crowns before thee,
Lost in wonder, love, and praise!

Mine eyes have seen the glory
Julia Ward Howe

Mine eyes have seen the glory of the coming of the Lord;
he is trampling out the vintage where the grapes of
   wrath are stored;
he has loosed the fateful lightning of his terrible swift
   sword:
his truth is marching on.

Glory, glory alleluia!
Glory, glory alleluia!
Glory, glory alleluia!
His truth is marching on.

He has sounded forth the trumpet that shall never call
   retreat;
he is sifting out the hearts of men before his
   judgement-seat:
O be swift, my soul, to answer him, be jubilant, my feet!
Our God is marching on.

Glory, glory alleluia!
Glory, glory alleluia!
Glory, glory alleluia!
Our God is marching on.

In the beauty of the lilies Christ was born across the sea,
with a glory in his bosom that transfigures you and me,
as he died to make men holy, let us live to make men free,
while God is marching on.

Glory, glory alleluia!
Glory, glory alleluia!
Glory, glory alleluia!
While God is marching on.

Nearer, my God, to thee

Sarah Flower Adams

Nearer, my God, to thee,
Nearer to thee!
E'en though it be a cross
That raiseth me,
Still all my song shall be:
'Nearer, my God, to thee,
Nearer to thee!'

Though, like the wanderer,
The sun gone down,
Darkness be over me,
My rest a stone;
Yet in my dreams I'd be
Nearer, my God, to thee,
Nearer to thee!

There let the way appear
Steps unto heaven -
All that thou sendest me
In mercy given -
Angels to beckon me
Nearer, my God, to thee,
Nearer to thee!

Then, with my waking thoughts
Bright with thy praise,
Out of my stony griefs
Bethel I'll raise;
So by my woes to be
Nearer, my God, to thee,
Nearer to thee!

Now is eternal life
G. W. Briggs

Now is eternal life,
If risen with Christ we stand,
In him to life reborn,
And holden in his hand;
No more we fear death's ancient dread,
In Christ arisen from the dead.

For God, the living God,
Stooped down to our estate;
By death destroying death,
Christ opened wide life's gate:
He lives, who died; he reigns on high;
Who lives in him shall never die.

Unfathomed love divine,
Reign thou within my heart;
From thee nor depth nor height,
Nor life nor death can part;
Our life is hid with God in thee,
Now and through all eternity.

Now thank we all our God

Martin Rinkart, trans. Catherine Winkworth

Now thank we all our God,
With hearts and hands and voices;
Who wondrous things hath done,
In whom his world rejoices;
Who from our mother's arms,
Hath blessed us on our way
With countless gifts of love,
And still is ours today.

O may this bounteous God
Through all our life be near us,
With ever joyful hearts
And blessèd peace to cheer us;
And keep us in his grace,
And guide us when perplexed,
And free us from all ills
In this world and the next.

All praise and thanks to God
The Father now be given,
The Son, and him who reigns
With them in highest heaven;
The One eternal God,
Whom earth and heaven adore;
For thus it was, is now,
And shall be evermore.

Now the green blade riseth
J. M. C. Crum

Now the green blade riseth from the buried grain,
Wheat that in dark earth many days has lain;
Love lives again, that with the dead has been:
  Love is come again,
  Like wheat that springeth green.

In the grave they laid him, Love whom men had slain,
Thinking that never he would wake again,
Laid in the earth like grain that sleeps unseen: Refrain

Forth he came at Easter, like the risen grain,
He that for three days in the grave had lain,
Quick from the dead, my risen Lord is seen: Refrain

When our hearts are wintry, grieving, or in pain,
Thy touch can call us back to life again,
Fields of our hearts, that dead and bare have been:
  Love is come again,
  Like wheat that springeth green.

O God, *our help in ages past*
Isaac Watts

O God, our help in ages past,
Our hope for years to come,
Our shelter from the stormy blast,
And our eternal home;

Under the shadow of thy throne
Thy saints have dwelt secure;
Sufficient is thine arm alone,
And our defence is sure.

Before the hills in order stood,
Or earth received her frame,
From everlasting thou art God,
To endless years the same.

A thousand ages in thy sight
Are like an evening gone,
Short as the watch that ends the night
Before the rising sun.

Time, like an ever-rolling stream,
Bears all its folk away;
They fly forgotten, as a dream
Dies at the opening day.

O God, our help in ages past,
Our hope for years to come,
Be thou our guard while troubles last,
And our eternal home.

O *Love that wilt not let me go*

George Matheson

O Love that wilt not let me go,
I rest my weary soul in thee;
I give thee back the life I owe,
That in thine ocean depths its flow
May richer, fuller be.

O light that followest all my way,
I yield my flickering torch to thee;
My heart restores its borrowed ray,
That in thy sunshine's blaze its day
May brighter, fairer be.

O joy that seekest me through pain,
I cannot close my heart to thee;
I trace the rainbow through the rain,
And feel the promise is not vain,
That morn shall tearless be.

O Cross that liftest up my head,
I dare not ask to fly from thee;
I lay in dust life's glory dead,
And from the ground there blossoms red
Life that shall endless be.

O *Strength and Stay upholding all creation*
St Ambrose, trans. John Ellerton

O Strength and Stay upholding all creation,
Who ever dost thyself unmoved abide,
Yet day by day the light in due gradation
From hour to hour through all its changes guide;

Grant to life's day a calm unclouded ending,
An eve untouched by shadows of decay,
The brightness of a holy death-bed blending
With dawning glories of the eternal day.

Hear us, O Father, gracious and forgiving,
Through Jesus Christ thy co-eternal Word,
Who, with the Holy Ghost, by all things living
Now and to endless ages art adored.

.

Praise, my soul, the King of heaven

H. F. Lyte

Praise, my soul, the King of heaven;
To his feet thy tribute bring.
Ransomed, healed, restored, forgiven,
Who like me his praise should sing?
Praise him! Praise him!
Praise the everlasting King.

Praise him for his grace and favour
To our forebears in distress;
Praise him still the same for ever,
Slow to chide, and swift to bless.
Praise him! Praise him!
Glorious in his faithfulness.

Father-like, he tends and spares us;
Well our feeble frame he knows;
In his hands he gently bears us,
Rescues us from all our foes.
Praise him! Praise him!
Widely as his mercy flows.

Angels, help us to adore him;
Ye behold him face to face;
Sun and moon, bow down before him;
Dwellers all in time and space.
Praise him! Praise him!
Praise with us the God of grace.

O thou who camest from above
Charles Wesley

O thou who camest from above,
The pure celestial fire to impart,
Kindle a flame of sacred love
On the mean altar of my heart.

There let it for thy glory burn
With inextinguishable blaze,
And trembling to its source return
In humble prayer, and fervent praise.

Jesus, confirm my heart's desire
To work, and speak, and think for thee;
Still let me guard the holy fire,
And still stir up thy gift in me.

Ready for all thy perfect will,
My acts of faith and love repeat,
Till death thy endless mercies seal,
And make my sacrifice complete.

Teach me, my God and King
George Herbert

Teach me, my God and King,
In all things thee to see;
And what I do in anything
To do it as for thee!

A man that looks on glass,
On it may stay his eye;
Or if he pleaseth, through it pass,
And then the heaven espy.

All may of thee partake;
Nothing can be so mean,
Which with this tincture, 'for thy sake',
Will not grow bright and clean.

A servant with this clause
Makes drudgery divine;
Who sweeps a room, as for thy laws,
Makes that and the action fine.

This is the famous stone
That turneth all to gold;
For that which God doth touch and own
Cannot for less be told.

The day thou gavest, Lord, is ended
John Ellerton

The day thou gavest, Lord, is ended,
The darkness falls at thy behest;
To thee our morning hymns ascended,
Thy praise shall sanctify our rest.

We thank thee that thy Church unsleeping,
While earth rolls onward into light,
Through all the world her watch is keeping,
And rests not now by day or night.

As o'er each continent and island
The dawn leads on another day,
The voice of prayer is never silent,
Nor dies the strain of praise away.

The sun that bids us rest is waking
Our kindred 'neath the western sky,
And hour by hour fresh lips are making
Thy wondrous doings heard on high.

So be it, Lord; thy throne shall never,
Like earth's proud empires, pass away;
Thy kingdom stands, and grows for ever,
Till all thy creatures own thy sway.

The King of love my Shepherd is
H. W. Baker

The King of love my Shepherd is,
Whose goodness faileth never;
I nothing lack if I am his
And he is mine for ever.

Where streams of living water flow
My ransomed soul he leadeth,
And where the verdant pastures grow
With food celestial feedeth.

Perverse and foolish oft I strayed,
But yet in love he sought me,
And on his shoulder gently laid,
And home, rejoicing, brought me.

In death's dark vale I fear no ill
With thee, dear Lord, beside me;
Thy rod and staff my comfort still,
Thy cross before to guide me.

Thou spread'st a table in my sight;
Thy unction, grace bestoweth:
And O what transport of delight
From thy pure chalice floweth!

And so through all the length of days
Thy goodness faileth never;
Good shepherd, may I sing thy praise
Within thy house for ever.

The Lord's my shepherd
Scottish Psalter 1650

The Lord's my shepherd, I'll not want;
He makes me down to lie
In pastures green; he leadeth me
The quiet waters by.

My soul he doth restore again,
And me to walk doth make
Within the paths of righteousness,
E'en for his own name's sake.

Yea, though I walk in death's dark vale,
Yet will I fear no ill:
For thou art with me, and thy rod
And staff me comfort still.

My table thou hast furnishèd
In presence of my foes;
My head thou dost with oil anoint,
And my cup overflows.

Goodness and mercy all my life
Shall surely follow me;
And in God's house for evermore
My dwelling-place shall be.

The strife is o'er, the battle done

Latin, seventeenth century, trans. Francis Pott

The strife is o'er, the battle done;
Now is the Victor's triumph won;
O let the song of praise be sung.
Alleluya!

Death's mightiest powers have done their worst,
And Jesus hath his foes dispersed;
Let shouts of praise and joy outburst.

On the third morn he rose again
Glorious in majesty to reign;
O let us swell the joyful strain.

He brake the age-bound chains of hell;
The bars from heaven's high portals fell;
Let hymns of praise his triumph tell.

Lord, by the stripes which wounded thee
From death's dread sting thy servants free,
That we may live, and sing to thee.

Thine be the glory
Edmond Budry

Thine be the glory, risen, conquering Son,
Endless is the victory thou o'er death hast won;
Angels in bright raiment rolled the stone away,
Kept the folded grave-clothes where thy body lay.
Thine be the glory, risen, conquering Son,
Endless is the vict'ry thou o'er death hast won.

Lo, Jesus meets us, risen from the tomb;
Lovingly he greets us, scatters fear and gloom;
Let the Church with gladness hymns of triumph sing,
For her Lord now liveth, death hath lost its sting: Refrain

No more we doubt thee, glorious Prince of Life;
Life is nought without thee: aid us in our strife,
Make us more than conquerors through thy deathless love;
Bring us safe through Jordan to thy home above:
Thine be the glory, risen, conquering Son,
Endless is the vict'ry thou o'er death hast won.

Thine for ever! God of love
Mary Maude

Thine for ever! God of love,
Hear us from thy throne above;
Thine for ever may we be
Here and in eternity.

Thine for ever! O, how blest
They who find in thee their rest!
Saviour, Guardian, heavenly Friend,
O defend us to the end.

Thine for ever! Lord of life,
Shield us through our earthly strife;
Thou the Life, the Truth, the Way,
Guide us to the realms of day.

Thine for ever! thou our guide,
All our wants by thee supplied,
All our sins by thee forgiven,
Led by thee from earth to heaven.

Acknowledgements

The publisher and author acknowledge with thanks permission to reproduce extracts from the sources listed here. Every effort has been made to seek permission to use copyright material reproduced in this book. The publisher apologizes for those cases where permission might not have been sought and, if notified, will formally seek permission at the earliest opportunity.

Unless otherwise noted, Scripture quotations are from the New Revised Standard Version of the Bible, Anglicized Edition, copyright © 1989, 1995 by the Division of Christian Education of the National Council of the Churches of Christ in the USA. Used by permission. All rights reserved.

Sophia de Mello Breyner Andresen, 'Quando'. English translation, 'When', by Margaret Jull Costa, copyright © 2014.

Vera Arlett, 'After I have gone', from *In Loving Memory*, edited by Sally Emerson, published by Little, Brown, 2004.

Simon Armitage, 'I thought I'd write my own obituary', from *Book of Matches*, published by Faber & Faber Ltd, 2001.

W. H. Auden, 'Funeral blues, from *The English Auden*, edited by Edward Mendelson, published by Faber & Faber Ltd, 2001.

W. H. Auden, 'If I could tell you', published by Random House, Inc., 1945. Copyright © 1945 by W. H. Auden.

Cardinal Joseph Bernardin, excerpt from *The Gift of Peace: Personal Reflections*, published by Loyola Press, 1977. Reprinted with permission of Loyola Press. <www.loyolapress.com>.

J. M. C. Crum (1872–1958), 'Now the green blade riseth' [altd.], from *Celebration Hymnal*. Reprinted by permission of Oxford University Press. All rights reserved.

Emily Dickinson, 'After great pain a formal feeling comes', from *The Poems of Emily Dickinson*, edited by Ralph W. Franklin, published by Harvard University Press, 1998.

Emily Dickinson, 'If I can stop one heart from breaking' ('Not in vain'), from *The Poems of Emily Dickinson*, edited by Thomas H. Johnson, published by The Belknap Press of Harvard University Press, 1983. Copyright © 1951, 1955 by the President and Fellows of Harvard College. Copyright © renewed 1979, 1983 by the President and Fellows of Harvard College. Copyright © 1914, 1918, 1919, 1924, 1929, 1930, 1932, 1935, 1937, 1942, by Martha Dickinson Bianchi. Copyright © 1952, 1957, 1958, 1963, 1965, by Mary L. Hampson.

Emily Dickinson, 'She died,–this was the way she died', from *In Memoriam: Poems of Bereavement*, published by Candlestick Press, 2012.

Douglas Dunn, 'Sandra's mobile', from *Elegies*, published by Faber & Faber Ltd, 2001.

Edna Eglinton, 'Attempts at the rational approach', from *The Nation's Favourite Poems of Remembrance*, published by BBC Books, 2008.

T. S. Eliot, from 'East Coker', from *Four Quartets*, published by Faber & Faber Ltd, 2001.

James Fenton, 'The ideal', from *Out of Danger*, published by Penguin, 1993.

Robert Frost, 'Nothing gold can stay', from *The Poetry of Robert Frost*, edited by Edward Connery Lathem, published by Jonathan Cape, 2001. Reprinted by permission of The Random House Group Ltd.

Norman MacCaig, 'Praise of a man', from *Collected Poems*, published by Chatto & Windus, 1990.

Louis MacNeice, 'Meeting point' and 'The sunlight on the garden', from *Collected Poems*, published by Faber & Faber Ltd, 2007.

Leo Marks, 'Code poem for the French Resistance', from *Between Silk and Cyanide: A Codemaker's War, 1941–1945*, published by HarperCollins Ltd, 1999.

A. A. Milne, from *The House at Pooh Corner*, in *Poems and Readings for Funerals* published by New Holland, 2009.

Edwin Muir, 'The way', from *The Complete Poems of Edwin Muir*, published by Association for Scottish Literary Studies, 1991.

Pablo Neruda, 'Sonnet LXXXIX', from *100 Love Sonnets*, translated by Stephen Tapscott, published by the University of Texas Press, 1986.

Alden Nowlan, 'This is what I wanted to sign off with', from *Between Tears and Laughter*, published by Bloodaxe Books, 2004.

Hugh O'Donnell', 'Light (for Ciaran)', from *Poems for Funerals*, edited by Neil Astley, published by Bloodaxe Books, 2003. Reprinted by kind permission of the author.

Mary Oliver, 'In Blackwater Woods', from *American Primitive*, published by Little, Brown, 1983, reprinted in *New and Selected Poems*, published by Beacon Press, 1992.

Mary Oliver, 'When death comes', from *New and Selected Poems*, published by Beacon Press, 1992. Copyright © 1992 by Mary Oliver. Reprinted by permission of The Charlotte Sheedy Literary Agency Inc.

– 230 –

Alice Walker, 'Good night, Willie Lee, I'll see you in the morning', from *Her Blue Body Everything We Know: Earthling Poems, 1965–1990 Complete*, published by The Women's Press Ltd, 1991. Reprinted by permission of David Higham Associates Ltd.

Anna Wigley, 'The baton', from *In Memoriam: Poems of Bereavement*, published by Candlestick Press, 2012.

Yakamochi, 'Only a little while' ('"We were together" by Yakamochi [XCVII]'), by Kenneth Rexroth, from *One Hundred Poems from the Japanese*. Copyright © 1955 by New Directions Publishing Corp. Reprinted by permission of New Directions Publishing Corp.

The author also thanks Ann Ruby for all her administrative help in compiling this book.